one child by choice

Sharryl Hawke, M.A., is Staff Associate of the Social Science Education Consortium, Boulder, Colorado. She is the author of numerous education publications and articles in magazines, including *Parents' Magazine* and *Family Health.*

David Knox, Ph.D., is Associate Professor of Sociology at East Carolina University, Greenville, North Carolina. He is the author of *Marriage: Who? When? Why?* (Prentice-Hall).

One Child
by Choice

Sharryl Hawke
David Knox

A SPECTRUM BOOK

Prentice-Hall, Inc., *Englewood Cliffs, N.J. 07632*

Library of Congress Cataloging in Publication Data

HAWKE, SHARRYL.
   One child by choice.

   (A Spectrum Book)
   Includes bibliographical references and index.
     1. Family size—United States. 2. Only child.
I. Knox, David, (date) joint author. II. Title.
HQ536.H38   301.42'7   77-9340
ISBN 0-13-634618-9
ISBN 0-13-634600-6 pbk.

© 1977 by Prentice-Hall, Inc., Englewood Cliffs, N.J. 07632

Printed in the United States of America

10 9 8 7 6 5 4 3 2 1

PRENTICE-HALL INTERNATIONAL, INC., *London*
PRENTICE-HALL OF AUSTRALIA PTY. LIMITED, *Sydney*
PRENTICE-HALL OF CANADA, LTD., *Toronto*
PRENTICE-HALL OF INDIA PRIVATE LIMITED, *New Delhi*
PRENTICE-HALL OF JAPAN, INC., *Tokyo*
PRENTICE-HALL OF SOUTHEAST ASIA PTE. LTD., *Singapore*
WHITEHALL BOOKS LIMITED, *Wellington, New Zealand*

Dedicated to our children,
Mark Hawke and Lisa Knox

Contents

Preface

The time for the one-child family has come. For too long parents and prospective parents have been persuaded by folklore that having an "only child" is not just a condition, but a near-fatal disease. Today's parents can no longer afford to accept this assessment without challenge. Overpopulation, inflation, dual-career marriages, and changing lifestyles call for a fresh look at the one-child family.

As parents of single children, we, the authors, are not against children. We love our children. We are against popular opinion and propaganda which suggest that a single child is doomed to maladjustment, that spouses must have at least two children before they qualify for full-fledged parenthood, and that members of a one-child family are neither normal nor happy. We do not believe that every couple should limit their family size to one. We do believe that every couple should objectively consider the benefits—and the drawbacks—of having a single child.

The book is divided into three parts. In Part I we examine the issues involved in deciding to become parents and in deciding to stop with one. Part II deals with rearing the single child, the adult single child, and the special situation of the single child reared by the single parent. Throughout the book we purposely use the term "single child" to avoid the negative connotations commonly associated with the traditional term "only child."

Although reflecting the research of previous studies, this book is based on original research with 750 nonrandomly selected people who participated in five separate studies over a four-year period (see Part III: Appendices). Participants were drawn from geographic areas throughout the nation and represent a broad spectrum of socioeconomic backgrounds. When warranted, we have changed names and identifying details to protect the anonymity of our participants. We are indebted to them for participating in the studies.

In preparing our book, we met many parents who expressed an interest in joining an organization dedicated to the one-child family. With the aid of Ellen Peck and others, we have formed the Association for the One-Child Family, a national, nonprofit organization. For further details on the Association, please turn to page 226.

SHARRYL HAWKE

DAVID KNOX

Introduction

Ask a young couple today how many children they plan to have, and you'll probably get one of two replies—"two" or "none."

"We're going to have two children" is the more likely of the two responses. Today, 35 per cent of all parents have or expect to have two children.[1] "It's the perfect family size," say many parents of two. "Two children are affordable. Each child has a built-in playmate, but the house isn't overflowing with kids. And having two gives you a chance to have a child of each sex." The two-child family is further promoted by mass media, which uses pictures of four-person families to sell everything from toothpaste to station wagons. It also receives the special blessing of population experts, who say that zero population growth (each parent replacing only himself/herself) is necessary if the world is to survive.

Although fewer couples decide to have no children, changing life-styles and spiraling inflation have made the childfree alternative more attractive to today's young adults. Couples who decide to remain childless find support for their decision in books such as *The Baby Trap* and *Mother's Day Is Over*, and even a group, the National Organization for Non-Parents. A couple who has chosen to be childfree may tell you, "We decided parenthood just doesn't fit our life-style. We have active careers, like to do things spontaneously, and really don't get that excited about kids. We're going to do our part for the world by not having children—children the world doesn't need anyway."

In the various discussions about family size, the statement you rarely hear is, "We're going to have one child." Only 10 per cent of married parents have or expect to have one child.[2] Apparently some of these parents have one child by default rather than choice, because only 2 per cent of people polled in a 1977 Gallup poll said that they thought one child was the "ideal" number of children.[3] In our society, the one-child family is simply not considered a desirable family size.

Because the one-child family has some obvious advantages, its lack of popularity is curious. With one child, parents can enjoy the rewards of parenthood without feeling overwhelmed by parental responsibilities. They can experience the pleasures of watching a child develop and share the special parent-child love relationship that the multichild parent enjoys. One child costs parents less, restricts them less (and for fewer years), minimizes the work load of child rearing, and holds the parents' impact on population growth below replacement level.

In view of these advantages, why don't more people have a one-child family? Why do so many couples today limit their considerations to "two children" or "no children"?

In talking with prospective parents over the past four years, we have heard two basic objections to the one-child family. One comes from couples who choose to have no children. They say that for them even one child is "too many." They don't believe the parenting experience is worth it, even once.

People who do want to become parents raise the opposite objection. "One child," they say, "is not enough." They contend that having one child is not fair to the child, that one child is not enough to experience parenthood fully, that something is "missed" when the family unit has only one child—in essence, they say there is something inherently "wrong" with having a single child.

In this book, we will address the concerns of both those who say one child is "too many" and those who say one child is "not enough."

one child by choice

one / *Deciding to Have One Child*

one / *Why Have a Child?*

If there were not two of us, the question of why
would never occur.[1]

B. F. Skinner

In a letter to her former college roommate, a young wife
expressed her concerns about parenthood:

> I'm turned off to parenthood because what I'm told about the joys
> of having children doesn't match up with what I see around me.
>
> I'm told, for instance, that children are the beautiful, healthy little
> muppets that pictures in *Parents' Magazine* and Johnson and Johnson
> commercials show us. But I have one friend whose daughter has an
> ugly birthmark on her face, another whose son has a congenital
> heart problem, and still another whose nine-year-old daughter can't
> read.
>
> I'm told that having children really won't change my life—only
> enrich it. Yet my acquaintances who are parents moan about vaca-
> tions missed because junior needed braces, the nights of sleep lost
> waiting for a teen-ager to get home safely, and the time spent patch-
> ing knees of an endless stack of jeans.
>
> I'm told that being a parent will make me a better person. But I've
> seen some of my friends change from spontaneous, fun-loving peo-
> ple to nervous, tired women who seem always to be living on the

3

edge. I have only to open my windows and listen to the screaming mothers in our apartment complex to question the assumption that parenthood automatically confers patience and compassion on a person.

I'm told that a child will bring my husband and me closer in our marriage. Perhaps. But in the past couple of years, three couples in our circle of friends have split either because the husband felt neglected by his wife's attention to their child and left her for another woman, or because the wife resented her husband's lack of interest in the child and decided to go it alone.

Finally, I'm told that even if rearing kids is a bother when they're young, parenthood pays off when they become adults. And yet I see my own parents going through hell because my younger brother took off for a commune two years ago and hasn't been heard from since. I also read that when Ann Landers asked her readers if they thought being a parent was worth it, 70 per cent of the 10,000 parents who wrote in said "no."[2]

In some ways I'd like to have a child. But as I see what happens when people have children, parenthood looks like more risk than I care to take.

The Folklore of Parenthood

Until recently, few people questioned the institution of parenthood as did the childfree wife in the above letter. Becoming a parent has been traditionally regarded as a "highlight of life's experiences," if not the "very meaning of life itself." It was considered the normal, logical postlude to marriage, and its benefits were thought to be self-evident.

Now more young couples are questioning the merits of parenthood, and many of them are concluding that much of what has been regarded as "truth" about parenting is half-truth at best and false at worst. E.E. LeMasters, a professor in the School of Social Work at the University of Wisconsin, calls the collection of statements that exaggerate the benefits and minimize the problems of child-rearing "the folklore" of parenthood. He writes, "When a social function is relatively difficult, as parenthood appears to be in our society, a romantic folklore develops to keep the role from being ignored or rejected by most adults."[3]

The folklore began to develop when society needed offspring to assure that the human species did not become extinct and to provide enough people to gather food, build shelter, and protect the aging. Those days are now past. The species is in no apparent danger of dying out (quite the opposite), and children, rather than being economic assets, are generally economic liabilities in this urban, inflationary age.

But the folklore lives on; indeed, it flourishes. Our parents tell us that we are "the pride and joy" of their lives, and they imply (or state) that becoming a grandparent will make them happier than anything else. Our friends who are parents encourage us to have children by suggesting that parenthood is the ticket to adulthood. "I wasn't a real woman until I had a baby," is a remark commonly directed to the childfree woman.

Less personal, but no less inspired, is the promotion of parenthood by the media, which shows us endearing scenes of families with spotless kids and floors to match. Religions tell us that parenthood is a spiritual experience. Our government gives us a tax deduction for producing children, and society adds its special inducement by celebrating Mother's and Father's days.

As with the folklore surrounding all institutions, the parenthood folklore and the pressure of those who expound it keep prospective parents from looking objectively at parenthood. Turned off by the obvious distortions of the folklore, some couples never look beyond the myths to discover that there are rewards in parenting—some very real and unique rewards.

Parenthood: An Experience Worth Having

"I've noticed when someone asks me what I think about being a mother, I usually come off pretty negative," confessed the mother of a year-old daughter. "Really I don't feel negative about it, but it's easier to count the dirty diapers or add up the doctor bills than to try to describe what it means to me when my child cuddles up on my lap or squeals with pleasure when Daddy comes home."

Trying to describe the rewards of parenthood is difficult. Because the rewards are often intangible, very personal, and seemingly self-evident, parents find it hard to pinpoint their positive feelings. Perhaps the elusive nature of parenting rewards has also steered researchers away from the task of determining what satisfactions mothers and fathers derive from the parenthood experience. In a thorough review of research on the consequences of parenting, Dr. Kenneth Terhune concluded, "Presumably the expectations of gratifications lead people to want children in the first place, yet despite all the research on the consequences of family size, we find no data to tell us whether those expectations are realized or not."[4]

By contrast, the drawbacks of parenting are usually easy to define and discuss. Costs, hours of lost sleep, loads of laundry, missed social activities, and interruptions can be counted and persuasively explained. However, because the rewards of parenthood are less tangible and less easily described than the drawbacks, we should not assume that they are less real or less important. Mothers and fathers we have questioned believe that there are rewards in parenting, and they name the following points as some of the most gratifying.

Children Themselves

Many parents believe that the greatest reward of parenting is children themselves. In a discussion group of middle-aged adults, the group leader once asked each participant to name the person who had been most influential in his or her life. Without hesitation, one father replied, "My son. He has touched my emotions, opened my eyes, and rejuvenated me in a way no adult ever has."

Appreciation of a child as a unique individual begins in the first years of parenting. Despite the frustrations of coping with the day-by-day, hour-by-hour demands of young chil dren, there is a certain magic about kids. Part of it is their spontaneity. Unlike adults who are burdened by years of social programming, a child responds freely to his or her environment from the "gut level." Much of the spontaneity is funny, as Art Linkletter aptly illustrates in his book *Kids Say the Darndest Things*. One of the activities that delights parents most (and bores nonparents most) is relating their child's latest flash of wit.

The young child's spontaneity can be sentimental as well as humorous. One night a five-year-old awakened, went into her parents' bedroom, put her arms around her mommy and daddy, kissed them and said "I love you." The parents slept well that night.

The young child is also honest. When a child says the meat loaf is good, you know it is. When a teen-ager tells you your slacks are unfashionably short, you know they are. Although the honesty of children can be disconcerting (and sometimes embarrassing), it is a welcome relief in an adult world of innuendo, false fronts, and social game playing.

For those who complain that they don't have enough energy, the perpetual motion of a young child is inspiring (although difficult to keep up with). A graduate student and father who was listless about completing his dissertation said, "My kids make me feel guilty for sleeping until ten. It's easier for me to get going when I see them running, laughing, teasing, throwing, and jumping. The energy they create is contagious and gets me off my duff."

Children are also great companions. "I wasn't too crazy about having a child," recalled a college professor, "and I certainly never thought I'd really enjoy having a child around. But I do. Especially now that he's in school, I think I would rather spend time with him than anyone else. I'm fascinated by the way he sees things, and the way he thinks and communicates about them. His mother says he's a lot like me. Maybe that's why I like him."

Unlike the adult who may require a European tour to lift a depression, a child finds happiness everywhere. The eyes of a young child open wide with amazement at the sight of Santa Claus, a ladybug, or a toy duck at the fair. The teen-ager is usually less demonstrative about his or her joys, but sharing the adolescent's excitement when receiving a first driver's license or going on a first date can be as "happy" for parents as for their child.

Although the spontaneity and unrestrained happiness of children fade as they take on more "adult" behavior, parents find new satisfactions in their maturing children. "Seeing my daughter turn into an attractive young lady with a pretty face and a delightful personality to match really makes me feel proud," says the mother of a college girl.

Another pleasure that often increases as the child matures is friendship. "The most satisfying part of parenting for me came after my son reached adulthood and I could enjoy him as a thinking, independent person," said the father of a re-cent college graduate. "I don't always agree with his views, in fact I don't agree with him most of the time, but it pleases me that he's turned out to be a thoughtful person." A mother remarked, "I have a lot of good friends, but I would rather spend the afternoon with my grown daughter than any of them."

Although childfree couples may acknowledge that many parents truly enjoy their children, they sometimes ask, "Is it necessary to go through the cost and frustrations of parent-hood just to enjoy interacting with children? Can't you get the same kind of pleasure by relating to someone else's children—maybe by being a teacher or just spending time with the neighborhood kids?" In reply, Patricia, a pediatric nurse and mother of one, said, "Sure you can enjoy some of the pleasures without having your own child. But it's always at a distance. Experiencing some of the 'lows' of being a mother makes the 'highs' even higher."

Fulfillment

Because our society places so much value on parenthood, parents experience a real sense of fulfillment when their child is born or adopted. They have satisfied an important social expectation and are rewarded with cigars and baby showers, which demonstrate that society believes their accomplishment is valuable.

For a person who has a strong need to be in the mainstream of life, becoming a parent may represent not just fulfillment, but an important part of his or her identity. "Before my son, Benny, was born," remembered one mother, "I wasn't anything special. My husband and I weren't getting along, I hated my job, and I sure wasn't famous. Now I know who I am." Another mother agrees, "My husband loves me, but my baby needs me."

Even for the woman who does not define herself strictly as a mother, having a child is fulfilling. "I never wanted to be only a mother," said Jeannie, a fashion designer, "but I definitely did want to have a child. I've had some very exciting experiences in the fashion world, but none topped the excitement of seeing my daughter for the first time. She has added immeasurably to my total life experience."

Pregnancy and childbirth are a particularly dramatic aspect of the fulfillment that mothers experience with parenthood. The drama results partly from the element of mystery involved in pregnancy, partly from a sense of culminating all those years of playing with dolls in childhood. It is not suprising that 86 per cent of first-time mothers in one study reported that they were "happy" when they learned of their pregnancy.[5]

The fulfillment of parenthood is not limited to women. Men too derive a sense of identification and satisfaction from fathering children—particularly male children. "Call it macho if you like," said one father, "but I got a real thrill when my child was born. Down deep I think a lot of men feel that becoming a father is the ultimate demonstration of masculinity."

Nonparents often contend that the initial fulfillment of having a baby pales with the last baby gift. Then, they say, parents spend the next 18 years asking, "What's so fulfilling about worry, work, and bills?" A career woman, and dedicated nonparent, commented, "It's not worth the drain on my time and energy to get a few baby booties and a dozen red roses. I'll get my roses by being a better wife or better accountant, and skip the booties."

Although admitting that not all of parenting is "fulfilling," parents generally agree that fulfillment continues throughout life. "It's true that I found it hard to feel 'fulfilled' when my child was young and I had to struggle with potty training, dressing and undressing, spilled milk, and temper tantrums. But my child has gotten more fulfilling to me every year. When he started to school, when he was bar mitzvahed, when he graduated from college—those events in his life were as fulfilling for me as for him. They told me I had done an important job well, and that's satisfying no matter how many other kinds of rewards you get in your life."

Personal Growth

"I love my kids," said the mother of teen-age sons, "but I love even more the growth my children have produced in me as a person. People always think of parenting in terms of what a parent does for a child, but the real giving may be what the child does for the parents."

With a child, parents learn to be providers. For an infant, they must provide constant care. They learn to detect the needs of the child, then respond by diapering, feeding, or just cuddling. For the older child, parents learn to provide direction and the emotional support that helps the child to meet the challenges of growing up.

Parents also learn to be teachers and guides. In his book *Childhood and Society*, Eric Erikson writes about "generativity," an interest in establishing and guiding the next generation, as an important function of parenting.[6] A child's mind begins as an empty attic, and parents play a major role in filling the attic with (hopefully) accurate, truthful, and useful information.

"My parents did me a disservice by loading my mind with a bunch of myths and fables," remarked Brad, an electrical engineer. "They told me that the doctor brought me in his little black bag, that blacks had the same opportunities as whites, and that only those who went to Sunday school and church were 'good people.' I've enjoyed teaching my child what I think is closer to the truth—that discipline is the key to success, that books advertising 'education made easy' are a joke, and that the cardinal rule of life should be 'no harm to others.' "

Sometimes parents acquire a whole new set of personal skills while rearing children—skills they might not have otherwise bothered to learn. A father who was widowed when his three children were small described how he learned (slowly and painfully) to cook. "While my wife was alive, I didn't even plug in the coffeepot. Had I not had the kids, I'm sure I would have just gone out to eat after her death. But with them I couldn't afford it, so I got out my wife's high school home economics book and started with page one. After a couple of years I really came to enjoy cooking, and even though I'm now remarried I continue to spend a lot of time in the kitchen. My new wife's delighted because she hates to cook."

A mother tells how she was persuaded by her kids to take up skiing. "My husband had been trying for years to get me to ski, but I just wouldn't try it. When my kids started skiing with him every weekend, I figured I could either learn how or I would be sitting home alone on weekends. Now skiing is one of the things I most enjoy in life, both with my kids and by myself."

Because children tend to push adults to their limits (and beyond), many parents believe that their patience and tolerance increase with the parenting experience. Those capacities sometimes have real payoffs, as Carol, a mother of six, discovered when she started looking for a job after her last child left home.

> Normally, a forty-nine-year-old woman with no previous work experience feels she has little to qualify her for work outside the home. I was turned down at a number of places before I finally applied at a big insurance company. When the personnel director looked at my application, she said, "You're the person I need for a particularly difficult job we have. The younger women we've tried in the position just couldn't handle it, but you'll be perfect."
>
> The "difficult job" was answering the complaint phone. That meant I was the first person to whom clients complained about problems with payments or charges. It was up to me to calm them down and direct them to the appropriate person in the office. The personnel director figured if I'd raised six kids without committing murder or going crazy, I'd be able to do this job. And she was right. I did well at the job.

If nothing else, kids help adults put their world into perspective. For a child, a car that won't start, a guest who drops in unexpectedly when the house is a mess, or a neighbor's dog that barks is not the monumental crisis it often is for an adult. A child's constant search for the "whys" of life can inspire adults to take a fresh look at their activities. Questions such as "Why do you have to finish your report today?" "Why does the garage have to be cleaned?" "Why do we have to have daddy's boss for dinner?" often compel a reassessment of the consequences (real and imagined) of fulfilling or not fulfilling traditional expectations—expectations that seem to go unchallenged in the adult world.

The contention that children produce growth in parents is greeted with skepticism by many nonparents. Listening to a mother describe how much she had matured by becoming a parent, a childfree woman was moved to say, "I'm sure parenting is a maturing experience. But so's the army, and I don't want to do that either." Other nonparents suggest that although parenting may help to develop certain kinds of qualities, those aren't the qualities they're interested in.

"My career is the most important thing in my life," said a junior executive in a stock brokerage firm. "If I had a child, I might develop more patience and learn how to get spit-up stains out of receiving blankets, but I don't particularly care if I know how to do those things. I do want to get better at predicting market trends and making persuasive presentations at director's meetings, and I think a child would make that kind of growth more difficult."

There are trade-offs in parenthood. Parents sometimes have to sacrifice or restrict certain kinds of growth for the opportunity to develop other qualities. Nonparents believe that the pay-offs are not sufficient to justify the sacrifices of parenthood, but many parents believe that they come out the winner in the trade-offs. "I wouldn't say I'm a 'better' person since I've become a parent," commented a mother of two, "but I do think I'm emotionally, and to a certain extent intellectually, a more fully developed person."

Marital Growth

Another traditional belief about parenthood, which nonparents dispute, is that having a child will improve a marriage. "My experience tells me the idea that a child can make marriage better is a bill of goods," declared a childfree husband. "I've never seen a bad marriage improve after a child was born, but I've seen lots of good marriages fall apart after a child's arrival." Researchers who have examined the effect of children on a marriage have found that some specific things happen in a parents' relationship when a child enters the family unit. For example, a baby reduces parents' communication time by half.[7] A child also reduces the amount of touching and looking between parents. Dr. Paul Rosenblatt of the University of Minnesota observed 440 couples, some with children and some childless, in public places. He concluded that couples with children were much less likely to touch, smile, and talk with each other than couples without children.[8]

If you doubt Rosenblatt's findings, do your own test by comparing the interaction of childfree couples in a "singles" restaurant with the behavior of couples with children in a family restaurant. You will probably observe much talking, touching, and eye contact between the childfree couples. But among the couples with children, most of the interaction will occur between parents and children rather than between the two adults.

It seems clear that having children does change the marriage relationship, but is the change positive or negative? Researchers who have tried to answer that question have reached contradictory conclusions. Some, such as E.E. LeMasters[9] and Dr. Everett Dyer,[10] found that the majority of couples in their studies felt a child represented a major crisis in their lives. Dr. Harold Feldman of Cornell University compared couples having an infant with childfree couples married some length of time. Among the 850 couples, those with a child showed less marital satisfaction than those without a child.[11]

Other researchers disagree. Dr. Candyce Russell surveyed 568 parents and found only six per cent of the husbands and eight per cent of the wives felt that their marriage had deteriorated since the birth of their children.[12] Eighty-six per cent of the couples in a project by Dr. Daniel Hobbs thought that their baby presented only a "slight" crisis for their marriage,[13] and in our study of first-time fathers, 75 per cent of the participants reported that their baby had no effect on their marriage, while 20 per cent indicated that their marriage had improved (Appendix 3).

Parents who believe their child produced a positive effect on their marriage often talk about the common focus that the child brought to their marriage. "Joe and I really didn't have a lot in common before our children were born," remarked Joy, a mother of three. "But sharing both the good and bad times of their growing up has provided a focus in our lives. Maybe we could have gotten the same togetherness with golf, or starting a business together, or something else, but the children added an important dimension to our relationship."

An unexpected reward of parenthood is often the pleasure of seeing your spouse in a new role. Describing her arrival home from the hospital with their first child, one mother said, "When I walked through the door into our living room, my eyes were flooded with multicolored balloons hanging everywhere. In the middle of the room was a sign reading, 'Welcome Home Jenny and Jeff.' I swelled with joy at my husband's pride, and regard that moment as the happiest of my life."

The appreciation that husbands and wives have for each other as parents often grows along with the kids. "My wife and I have some pretty serious differences of opinion about several things," said a salesman and father of three, "but I have undying respect for her as a mother. She has raised our sons almost single-handedly because I'm on the road all the time, and she's done a remarkable job. I never thought much about what kind of mother she would be, but she's fantastic. I wish I'd had her as a mother."

Couples who have a baby in a last-ditch effort to save their marriage will probably find that the effort fails. However, if the couple has a good relationship before becoming parents, adding a child to that relationship can bring new joys and dimensions to their marriage. "Just seeing my husband with our kids makes it all worthwhile for me," concluded Marilyn, a mother of two. "It sounds corny, but it's true."

Link with Past and Future

A group of childfree couples at a social gathering were good-naturedly challenging the only father in the group to explain why he had deserted their cause to become a parent.

"Well, you're not going to believe this," replied the father, "but I wanted to have a child to carry on the family name. I'm the only son on my father's side of the house, and I truly felt a responsibility to keep the family tree alive. With the birth of my son, I feel I'm keeping up our family heritage."

A strong sense of family heritage compels many people to have a child. For other prospective parents, the family tradition is less important than their personal desire to have a part of them extend into the future. "Accepting life's temporariness is difficult for me," confided a new father. "By having a child, I feel I can extend my time frame a bit."

Having a child can also provide a link with the past. "My dad and I were never really close until David was born," remarked Fred as he watched his 18-month-old child. "Because I'm so intrigued with children right now, I really enjoy talking with my father about what I was like as a baby and what part he played in my early life. It pleases him that I'm interested, and I think it makes him happy to think about his experiences as a young man."

Identifying with their own parents on a new level is a bonus discovered by some new parents. In our study of first-time fathers, 10 per cent said their relationship with their own parents had improved after they had a child. The same per cent reported their relationship with in-laws had improved, sometimes to their amazement (Appendix 3). "When Jenny was born, my in-laws accepted me for the first time," said one new father. "I guess they thought since I'd had a part in producing that lovely grandchild, the least they could do was treat me like part of the family."

Is linking yourself with the past and the future a sound reason for having a child? Nonparents think not. They point out that there are other ways of establishing a niche in the future—creating a piece of art or literature, for example. Childfree advocates also ask why people feel they must "live on." "Why can't you just be satisfied with the time you have here and skip that future generation stuff?" asked a nonparent.

For persons who are not particularly interested in connections with the past or future, having a child will not stir a strong sense of tradition. But for those people who do see themselves as part of the progression of time and generations, parenting a child can be philosophically, as well as emotionally, rewarding.

Love

"You're trying to make it too logical and academic," said a friend when we told him that we were writing about the rewards of parenthood. "The real reward—the big payoff —is being able to love, and hopefully be loved by your own child. Admittedly, you have to put up with some crap to have that love, but it's such a special love that it makes the whole parenthood experience worthwhile."

The 102 first-time fathers in our study agree with this father's assessment. When asked to describe their feelings toward their child on a descriptive scale, every father chose the words "love" or "love plus extreme happiness" (Appendix 3).

And so there are rewards in parenting. They are not always easy to describe. They are not constant. They are different for each parent. But they are real, and they are persuasive enough to convince 92 per cent of adult Americans

that parenthood is a special experience, an experience that is
indeed worth having.[14]

Parenthood: An Experience Worth Repeating?

Having decided to have one child, parents confront a new
issue—"Shall we have a second child?" By having one child,
they have concluded that parenthood is an experience worth
having. Now they must decide if it is also an experience
worth repeating.

To make that decision, parents must answer several questions: Is being a single child fair to a child? Is having a single
child fair to the parents? What are the differences between
having one child and having more? Is the one-child family
really a desirable life-style? It is these questions we will discuss in the following chapters.

two / *Having One Child*
– Is It Fair
to the Child?

We had our first child because we wanted it. We
had our second child to save the first.

A MOTHER OF TWO

"In all honesty I'd have to say that we really didn't want to
have a second child," concluded Sharon, the mother of two
boys. "But we didn't think it was *fair* to our first son to grow
up as an only child."

Like Sharon and her husband, many people in our society
believe that children who don't have brothers and sisters are
disadvantaged. When a cross section of Americans were
asked in a Gallup poll if they thought that being an only child
was an advantage or disadvantage, 71 per cent said it was a
disadvantage, 20 per cent said it was an advantage, and nine
per cent didn't know.[1] This view was echoed in our study of
130 college students. Eighty-eight per cent of the students
felt that it was better to have a sibling than to be a single child
(Appendix 5). One student underscored his conviction with
the statement, "An only child is like a basketball without a
basket."

The widespread belief that a single child is disadvantaged
motivates many couples to have a second child. In a 1973

national sample survey, Janet Griffith found that 71 per cent of the women and 57 per cent of the men polled felt that it "would be bad for the child" if they had an only child.[2] When 239 couples were asked in an earlier study why they had a second child, the second most often cited reason was "not wanting to have an only child."[3]* A biologist we interviewed summed up this feeling when he said, "We didn't have any evidence to prove that an only child would be at a disadvantage. We just didn't want to take a chance."

Even present-day concerns about population growth and economic conditions are not increasing the popularity of the one-child family. In 1945 one per cent of Americans told Gallup pollsters that they considered one child the ideal family size;[4] among their counterparts in 1977 that figure had risen to only two per cent.[5] Our society has pronounced the single child "disadvantaged" and the one-child family "undesirable." The message has not been ignored. Today only 10 per cent of all American parents have, or expect to have, one child.[6]

The Negative View of Single Children

It is difficult to pinpoint when or why our negative view of single children originated. It may date back to a time when families and communities needed large families to assure survival. One child in a family was valuable, but more children were more valuable. Having many children was a status symbol for parents and provided them respect as well as enough hands to carry out the tasks of day-to-day living.

The need for many children in a family has long since passed, and smaller families have become more "respectable" than large ones. Yet the negative view of single children continues. Why? One reason is the influence of some turn-of-the-century research psychologists who delivered the earliest

*The first reason given was the "desire to insure against childlessness."

professional opinion on children raised without siblings.

The first of these opinions came from E.W. Bohannon, a psychologist who conducted research on single children in the late 1880s. After analyzing teachers' reports on 381 single children, Bohannon firmly concluded that these children were unhealthy, nervous, below average in academics, socially immature, selfish, and overindulged.[7] Although researchers today question the reliability of Bohannon's conclusions, his findings were generally accepted at the time. It was his work, plus that of the other early researchers, which led Dr. G. Stanley Hall, an eminent psychologist of the day, to write, "Being an only child is a disease in itself."[8] This statement was to be quoted frequently and almost without challenge for the next 30 years.

The impact of Bohannon, Hall, and others was not limited to the academic world. Popular magazines of the day reported the psychologists' findings to the general public in a variety of articles on the single child. Among the most influential was one that appeared in a 1927 issue of *Liberty* magazine. The article strongly warned readers about the dangers of "onliness," and its message was reinforced with an illustration showing a child seated on a throne with a scepter in hand and two miniature parents looking on in obvious submission.[9]

After the flurry of studies early in this century, there was a lull in research on single children until the late 1930s and 40s when a new guard of psychologists and sociologists revived interest in the subject. The work by these researchers generally showed single children in a much more favorable light than the earlier research. Gone were the firm declarations about the disadvantages of being a single child, and in their place was evidence that the single-child situation might have some distinct advantages. But these studies never received the media coverage the earlier studies had enjoyed. Few articles appeared in popular magazines, and only one book dealing with the single child was published. Consequently, despite the new evidence, the earlier negative reports on single children continued to dominate American thinking.

Although professional opinion has contributed to the public's view of single children, it only partly explains the persistent belief that single children are disadvantaged. Many people holding this point of view have never read or heard a professional opinion on single children. Their beliefs are based not on what the "experts" have said, but on their own experiences with single children and one-child families.

In preparing this book, we asked scores of people to give us their opinion of single children. Most said that they believed single children are disadvantaged or handicapped. When asked why, respondents nearly always began their answer by saying, "I know an only child, and he/she is. . ." The descriptions which followed were generally negative and tended to suggest one of two personality types: the "spoiled brat" or the "shrinking violet."

Single children in the spoiled brat category were characterized by our respondents as demanding, selfish, conceited, tempermental, uncooperative, and unpopular. "Only children never have to give and take," said one college student. "They just take, take, take." "Shrinking violets," on the other hand, were described as timid, overdependent, shy, unassertive, "lacking backbone," easily intimidated, and socially hesitant. As an elementary teacher commented, "Only children don't get in on the rough-and-tumble of life with brothers and sisters, so they never learn to stand up for themselves." These kinds of personal observations have convinced many people in our society that single children are destined "for trouble," or as one woman said, "only children are bound to be a mess."

The negative view of single children has a long tradition in our society. It has been perpetuated by both professional opinion and personal experience, and it is firmly adhered to by the vast majority of Americans. Is the view deserved? Are the beliefs about single children justified?

Single Children: The Myths

The remainder of this chapter will focus on what is myth and what is reality about the single child. Drawing definitive conclusions is difficult because recent research on single children is relatively limited, and the quality of earlier research is often questionable. However, by combining past research on single children with the results of our own study of 273 single children and one-child parents, we can examine the accuracy of many common beliefs about the "plight" of the single child. First the myths.

Single Children Are Spoiled and Selfish

The most enduring belief about single children maintains that they are self-centered, selfish, and spoiled. "I once had a friend who was an only child," commented Marty when asked about single children. "For years I did favors for her, listened to her problems, even loaned her money. Then one time I was seriously ill and really needed her help for a couple of days. She turned me down because she had a 'hot' date. I think only children become so self-centered in childhood that they're never able to extend themselves to others as adults."

Several studies in the past 50 years have attempted to determine if single children are more "spoiled" than other children. In 1927 the teachers of 350 kindergarten children were asked to rate each child's willingness to share. The completed ratings showed no difference between single children and children with siblings in possessiveness or sharing.[10] Findings of this early study were supported in 1959 when Britomear Handlon and Patricia Gross studied the sharing behavior of children in early elementary grades. Although age made a difference in the child's willingness to share, the size of family from which the child came seemed to have no influence—the single children shared just as well as children with siblings.[11] Refia Uğural-Semin did find more selfishness among children without siblings than children from larger families, but in his report he carefully points out that generosity is affected not just by family size, but also by age and socioeconomic class.[12]

In our interviews we asked parents of single children if they had observed more selfishness in their child than his or her friends with siblings. A few parents reported selfishness as one of their child's major problems, but many others described just the opposite situation. As one mother of an adult son explained, "Our problem with Matt was not that he was selfish, but that he was too generous. Since there was no one in competition with him for his toys, he didn't have to be selfish. We had to teach him that things didn't grow on trees and that he couldn't just give away his possessions."

Dr. Toni Falbo approached the question of selfishness in another way with a group of college students. She asked her subjects to participate in a game that required cooperation and trust, and she assessed their behavior during game play. Her conclusion? She found that single children were more likely than siblings to be cooperative and trusting when responding to a cooperative move by another player. She concluded, ". . .people who grow up without constant competition from other children in the family learn to trust the motives of other people. They don't have to worry about siblings who look lovingly at them while stealing their candy."[13]

Neither the results of experimental studies nor the reports of one-child parents confirm the persistent belief that single children are inevitably more spoiled than children with siblings. Many conditions contribute to a child's "spoiling." Onliness is not the "only"—perhaps not even the critical —factor.

Single Children Are Overly Dependent

"My best friend in grade school was an only child," recalled one interviewee. "We went everywhere together because she was so shy she hated to face people by herself. She wouldn't even go to school if I happened to be sick."

This "shrinking violet" description typifies the common belief that single children are inclined to be overly dependent. Dependency is the most extensively studied aspect of onliness, and the research results are clear. Single children, rather than being clinging vines, are more self-confident and independent than people having siblings.

In an early study by Ruth Guilford and D.A. Worchester, single children in kindergarten classes were rated by teachers as more self-confident than their peers.[14] Thirty-five years later Morris Rosenberg found that 51 per cent of the single children in a group of adolescents were high in self-esteem, while only 44 per cent of adolescents with siblings showed the same characteristic. Rosenberg concluded that "as far as self-esteem is concerned. . .the advantages [of being a single child] appear to outweigh the disadvantages."[15]

Research on adult single children is limited, but Dorothy Dyer found college-age single children to be slightly better adjusted than other students in the home and emotional areas of a personality adjustment inventory. She found nothing to indicate that these young adults were more dependent on their parents than other students when they left the home setting.[16] After reviewing all the research on dependency for his government report on consequences of family size, Dr. Kenneth Terhune concluded that on the balance, studies tend to support the view that dependency is a large-family manifestation, not a characteristic of single children.[17]

Sixty-five per cent of the adult single children we interviewed and 38 per cent of the young single children named self-confidence as an advantage of being reared in a one-child family (Appendix 1). Kathy, a 12-year-old, remarked, "Lots of my friends who have brothers and sisters worry about whether their parents like them as much as they do the other kids in the family. I'm glad I don't have to worry about that. I know I'm loved and that my parents will always stick up for me."

Of course, not every single child develops a healthy self-concept. Some single children, despite their onliness, receive little or no encouragement from parents. Others are so smothered with attention that it becomes intimidating. But, in general, research indicates that, as a group, single children are not predisposed to a poor self-concept or dependency —rather, they are much more likely to become self-confident, independent individuals.

Single Children Are Lonely

The "lonely only child" is a phrase often used to describe children from one-child families. A recent children's book, *Why Couldn't I Be An Only Kid Like You, Wigger*, attempts to show readers the good and bad aspects of life in different family sizes. The illustrations portraying Wigger, a single child, focus heavily on his loneliness—no one around to share his Christmas gifts (not even parents), dinner with adults (in dress clothes), and shopping with mother (for fabric). The point is clear—Wigger is lonely.[18]

How accurate is the picture of Wigger? Some research indicates that it is seriously distorted. Dr. Falbo assessed the loneliness of college students by asking them how many friends and close friends they had, how much time they spent by themselves daily, and how popular they felt. She found no differences between single children and siblings in their self-evaluations. According to Dr. Falbo, "the onlys were not visibly more likely to brood, friendless and alone, in their rooms."[19]

Other studies on popularity support Dr. Falbo's conclusions. One of the most thorough and often quoted studies on popularity among children was conducted by Merl E. Bonney during the 1940s. Studying elementary school children, Bonney set out to determine what relationships existed between popularity and family size, socioeconomic background, and intelligence. Although he found a strong tendency for more popular children to come from small families, his most dramatic finding was that only children were consistently rated the most popular by their peers.[20] Dr. Terhune summarized all the available data on "sociability" of people from different family sizes by saying that single children, and perhaps individuals from small families generally, are shown to be "more socially outgoing and socially accepted by their peers, than are their large-family counterparts."[21]

The subjects of popularity and loneliness were discussed by many of the single children we interviewed. Marge, a single child in her thirties who is married to a man from a family of eight children, provided an important insight. "When I was a kid," explained Marge, "I really worked at having friends and being popular. Since I didn't have any other kids at home for companionship, I had to go out and make friends, and I learned to really value friendships. Because my husband had seven brothers and sisters at home, he had no need to make friends outside his family. As a result, today he's much less outgoing than I and still looks to his family for most of his social activities."

Are single children lonely? Undoubtedly all single children experience some periods of loneliness. But so do children with siblings. Strong evidence showing that single children tend to have good social skills and to be popular with their peers indicates that loneliness is not generally a problem for single children.

Single Children Are Underachievers

"When I was in high school, there were three only children in my group of friends," recalled a father of two children. "All three of those guys were smart, but they were lazy as could be. Didn't make good grades, goofed off all the time. Two of them started to college, but didn't finish. The other one didn't even start, although his parents had plenty of money. I always thought that because they didn't have any competition at home with brothers or sisters they just didn't develop much ambition."

The belief that single children are inclined to underachieve is common. Some people maintain that it is lack of competition and stimulation from siblings. Others feel that the problem is more often parents who spoil and overprotect their single children. Is the belief valid? Do single children rank below siblings in intellectual ability and achievement?

One question that always arises about single children is how they rate with other children in intellectual capacity. A number of studies have compared the IQs of single children with children having siblings, but the results have not been consistent. Some studies have found single children, as a group, to have higher IQs than other children. These studies show that IQ decreases as family size increases.[22] Other studies, particularly a recent study of 81,000 twelfth-grade students, have found that single children rank below children from two- and sometimes three-child families in intellectual ability.[23]

John G. Claudy, who reported the findings of the study on twelfth graders, speculated that the explanation for the single children's ranking might lie in a theory of Robert M. Zajonc and Gregory B. Markus, who maintain that single children, like youngest children in a larger family, show lower intellectual abilities because they lack an important component in intellectual development—having a younger sibling to "teach." Without the opportunity to teach younger siblings (an activity that helps to clarify the "teacher's" thinking), intellectual ability is somewhat retarded.[24]

For now there is no clear answer as to how single children compare in intellectual capacity with children having siblings. They are not consistently below children with siblings; neither are they consistently above. Because factors other than family size are known to affect IQ, it may be impossible to make a direct cause-effect link between onliness and intellectual ability.

One aspect of achievement which does seem clearly related to being a single child is language ability. When Dr. Edith Davis studied five-, six-, and nine-year-old children, she found that single children were definitely superior in nearly all aspects of language development to their peers who had siblings.[25] This superior language ability is thought to result from a single child's more constant association with adults. Studies supporting this explanation show that children learn more from adults than from other children, despite the common belief that children are the best teachers of other children. A first-grade teacher observed, "Children trade limited vocabularies and knowledge among themselves. It's from contact and conversation with adults that their words and minds grow."

The language ability of single children may influence their school grades—another aspect of achievement. In studies on school grades, firstborn children often have been found to make better grades than later-borns, but in at least one study which distinguished between firstborns and single children, the single children made even better grades than the other firstborns.[26] Limited research on college students shows that single children do as well as others in college.[27] A British study found that a greater proportion of single children graduated from universities than children from other family sizes,[28] and at the University of Minnesota, single children were found to become successively more overrepresented at higher academic levels.[29]

The research on the achievement of single children is scattered and somewhat inconsistent, but there is no indication that as a group single children are less likely to achieve than children with siblings. Many factors contribute to the intellectual success of children. Although the single child lacks siblings to stimulate certain kinds of learning, he or she gains from the extra parental attention given most single children. This attention can pay off, according to a teacher with 25 years of experience.

"My years in the classroom have convinced me that the children who do best in school are those whose parents value academic success and take time to encourage their child to do well in school," says Ms. Roberts. "The only children I know generally have this kind of parent encouragement."

Single Children Are Maladjusted

"All the onlies I know either have problems or are problems," declared a father of six. His statement reflects a common belief that single children are likely to be poorly adjusted (at best) or emotionally disturbed (at worst). The issue greatly concerns parents and prospective parents of a single child. "I'd like to stop with this one," said the mother of a two-year-old, "but I'm afraid he won't be well adjusted if he's an only child."

Several researchers have tackled the question of single children's emotional stability by studying groups of "normal" children and adults. They found no difference or "negligible" differences in the emotional adjustment of single children and those who have siblings, at all age levels.[30] Other researchers working in guidance clinics and mental institutions have compared single children and those with siblings in these "abnormal" populations. Their findings vary. One team concluded that the one-child family situation contributed significantly to the emotional problems of only children admitted to their clinic.[31] However, J.A. Levy arrived at a different conclusion after studying 700 children in Chicago guidance clinics. He maintained that "the distribution of children's behavior problems appeared to have little relation to family size."[32]

Dr. Falbo, in her work with college students, rated the subjects with two scales of personality adjustment, one measuring extroversion/introversion and another measuring neuroticism. She found that birth order made no difference in how the students scored—single children were no more neurotic or unhappy than anyone else. However, Dr. Falbo did find that students who had siblings themselves *believed* that single children are more maladjusted.[33]

Within everyone's experience, there seems to be a single child who is clearly a problem—to him- or herself or to others. But there are children from two-child, three-child, and ten-child families who also are problems. Family size alone does not determine personality adjustment. After reviewing the available literature on personality and family size, Dr. Terhune concluded, "The only child, it seems, is more maligned than maladjusted."[34]

Single Children Are Unhappy

"Only children are sad children," commented a mother of two children in one of our studies. "They miss one of life's great experiences by not having a brother or sister, and it shows in their general outlook on life." Like this mother, many people contend that single children are discontented with their lot in life.

Although we did not ask single children if they were "happy," we did ask if they thought there were advantages in being a single child. Every respondent under age 18 answered "yes," and 86 per cent of the single-child adults agreed. When asked if there were disadvantages in being a single child, 65 per cent of the young single children and 75 per cent of the adults said "yes" (Appendix 1). In the view of single children, the "goods" of the one-child family seem to outweigh the "bads."

An architect who is a single child captured the feelings of

many single children we interviewed in this statement: "I don't know why people pity an only child so much. Sure there are some disadvantages, but don't middle children, and youngest children, and all others have certain disadvantages in their family positions? Being an only child poses certain problems, but I'd just as soon deal with those problems as others."

Single Children: The Realities

Although some of the common beliefs about single children are not supported by evidence, there are other dimensions of onliness that research and experience indicate are true.

Single Children Have More Possessions and Opportunities

"You get more things when you're an only child," observed Linda, a nine-year-old single child. All observation confirms this child's opinion. Single children not only have more material possessions than children with siblings, they also tend to have more experience opportunities. At least this is true for children within the same socioeconomic class.

How do single children regard their affluence? Those in our study were very aware of their material advantage and considered it a positive aspect of the one-child family. One-third of both the adult and young single children we surveyed cited "more possessions and opportunities" as the greatest benefit of onliness (Appendix 1). The youngsters frequently mentioned having a room of their own as an important possession that might be denied them if they had siblings. Adults pointed to travel experiences, musical instruments, educational opportunities, and, in one instance, "no division of my parents' estate" as rewards of having no siblings. Laura, who grew up during the Depression on a small Kansas farm, said, "My parents didn't have much money during those days, but I had more clothes and spending money than most of my friends because what my parents had didn't have to be divided."

Does this abundance of material advantages "spoil" a single child? The research cited earlier indicates that it does not, and this view was confirmed by the single children we interviewed. Few believed their possessions had posed a problem for them—either in childhood or adult life. The respondents who described themselves as "spoiled" (their own choice of words) attributed the problem not to the possessions themselves, but to the motivation of their parents in giving the gifts. These single children said that their parents had given gifts to "buy me off" or to "buy my affection."

The single child is likely to be well provided for. Whether material advantages are beneficial or detrimental depends not on the possessions themselves, but on the way in which they are given. When wisely provided, material possessions and opportunities can be an early advantage to a child and give him or her an edge throughout life.

Single Children Receive More Parental Attention

"Last week I kept my girl friend's son for three days. Ted is three and my son is five, so I had a chance to see what it would be like to have a second child. The biggest difference between having one and having two seemed to be the amount of undivided time I had with my child. My son and I both became frustrated because it seemed we could never finish a conversation or a task without interruption."

The observation of this mother can be readily confirmed by comparing the daily life in a one-child family with that in a multichild family. Single children simply receive more attention from their parents than those with siblings. This does not imply that a single child cannot be neglected—indeed, there are some poignant cases of woefully neglected single children. Neither does it imply that parents with more than one child do not give their children adequate attention. It does mean that parents of a single child have more time and energy to devote to that child.

Parental attention can be a mixed blessing. When apportioned in reasonable amounts, it can build self-confidence, a sense of security, a wide-ranging curiosity, and a deep affection between child and parents. When parental attention is extreme, it can smother a child and cause him or her to become overdependent or to reject the parents as a source of strength.

The single children we interviewed often mentioned the double-edged nature of parental attention. When asked to name advantages of onliness, nearly one-third of the single children mentioned "more parental attention" as a major advantage of being a single child (Appendix 1). However, when asked to cite problems of onliness, approximately the same percentage named "parental attention" as a major disadvantage.

In discussing the disadvantages of parental attention, single children had some specific complaints, such as "parents were too protective," "parents expected too much," "parents were too strict," and "parents pried too much." The important word in their reporting was "too." The onlies were not objecting to the overabundance of these behaviors. Lynn, a precocious eight-year-old girl, made this observation: "I like being an only child because I get all the goodies. But I also get all my parents' gripes. Sometimes I wish I had a brother or sister just so mom and daddy would have someone else to think about."

In dealing with the issue of parental attention in their book *The Only Child*, Norma Cutts and Nicholas Moseley write, "There is really no such thing as loving a child too much, but one can certainly manifest that love unwisely."[35] Parental attention, like material possessions, generally is provided a single child in abundance. *How* the attention is given is the key to its being advantageous or destructive to the child.

Single Children Miss the Pleasures–and Detriments–of Siblings

By definition, a single child has no brothers or sisters, and many people believe this condition is the most depriving aspect of being a single child. "My sister is, and always has been, a very important person in my life," explained a mother when discussing her motivation for having a second child. "I simply don't think it would be fair for me to deprive my child of the chance for that same kind of relationship."

The single children in our study were very aware of their lack of siblings and what this meant to them. When asked if there was ever a time when they wished to have a sibling, 64 per cent of the adult respondents replied "yes." About one-third reported that they most wanted a sibling when they were between the ages of 6 and 10—the years when many schoolmates' families were adding more children. Another third said that they most wanted a sibling in adolescence. Interestingly, 37 per cent of the single children wished for a brother, while 21 per cent wished for a sister (Appendix 1).

In describing what they felt they missed by not having siblings, the single children referred most often to the lack of companionship (Appendix 1). They also talked about lacking a "sense of family," which they often related to having large family gatherings on holidays and having someone with whom to share family experiences. Some even indicated that they regretted not having someone to "fight with."

In interviewing single children, we were impressed with the picture the respondents had in their minds of what it would be like to have a brother or sister. Almost to a person they pictured a warm, supportive relationship in which siblings genuinely liked each other (despite occasional "fights") and came to each other's defense in times of trouble. They regretted missing the experience of a close, healthy relationship.

The point overlooked by the respondents is that sibling relationships are not always close or healthy. In our study of 130 college students who had siblings, 36 per cent spoke of jealousy and rivalry as a problem in their relationship with their brothers or sisters. Another 22 per cent mentioned arguments and fighting as a difficulty in their families (Appendix 5). Sometimes differences in personality, interests, and age cause siblings to be indifferent or plainly hostile to each other. Thirty-nine per cent of the siblings in our study said there were times they had wished to be a single child (Appendix 5).

Although the majority of single children we surveyed expressed some regret in not having a sibling, their remorse was not total. In weighing the pros and cons of being a single child, many said they appreciated "being able to develop in an uncompetitive atmosphere," "not having to live up to an older brother or sister," "having a quiet household," "being able to make plans independently," and, as one adolescent noted, "not having to babysit with younger kids."

Should the child without siblings be pitied or envied? Neither. Certainly a single child misses some positive aspects of sibling relationships, but he or she also misses some of the detriments. Elizabeth Hurlock, a child development specialist, writes, "only children, spared most. . .sibling relationship problems, generally make better adjustments to school, teachers, and classmates. In addition, they usually have better relationships with their parents than children with siblings.[36]

Single Children Are More Adultlike

"As far back in my childhood as I can remember, I was a miniature adult," recalled Martha, a single child, now a medical technician. "My parents could take me anywhere and know I would not embarrass them. I couldn't begin to do that with my own two kids."

Findings of several studies suggest that, like Martha, most single children are more adultlike than children of the same age who have siblings. Firstborns are generally more adult-oriented than later-born children, but the tendency is even more noticeable in single children.[37] Because of their constant interaction with parents, single children often adopt the vocabularies and mannerisms of these two adults; they relate primarily to adults, whereas children with siblings relate primarily to other children. Such phrases as "the price of groceries," "Walter Cronkite," and "I'll have a cocktail" are those to which a single child is most often exposed. A child with siblings is more likely to be familiar with "Gimme my big wheel" or "Finders keepers."

In addition, single children are exposed more often to the adult social world than are children with siblings. Many single children we interviewed reported that their parents involved them at a young age in adult activities—concerts, dining out, sports events, cocktail parties, travel. As a result, they learned early in life how to behave and function in the adult world.

Being proficient in adult society can be an advantage to a child. It can lead to experiences and opportunities that other children seldom, or never, have. It can also result in a situation described by child development specialist Eda LeShan. "Because of their intense association with adults," writes Dr. LeShan, "some only children seem to develop a pseudo-sophistication—they develop a remarkably adult vocabulary at an early age and seem to have a wisdom beyond their years."[38]

This pseudo-sophistication can pose a hazard for the single child. When a child typically behaves in an adultlike manner, parents and other adults come to expect a level of behavior that is really beyond the child's chronological age. At some point the child inevitably "blows it." Whether it's a three-year-old talking aloud at a concert or a teen-ager coming to a formal dinner party in cut-off jeans, adults tend to be horrified when their adultlike only child behaves less maturely than they have come to expect.

When parents avoid expecting behavior which is beyond their child's chronological age, they can enjoy the times when the child is able to move in the adult world with ease, and their child can profit from the experiences. The ideal situation is one described by an adult single child in recalling her childhood. "When I wanted to be grown up, my parents let me do adultlike things. But if I just felt like being a kid, they didn't bug me. It was a super arrangement."

Being a Single Child—Is It Fair to the Child?

This chapter began with the question, "Is it fair to a child to be a single child?" Although the research reported does not give an unchallengeable answer, it does show that being a single child is not a decided disadvantage. If anything, the research indicates that onliness may be advantageous. One child development scholar, Arthur Jersild, goes a step further in stating that single children are in fact "juvenile VIPs."[39]

Being a single child—like being an oldest, middle, or youngest—has inherent advantages and disadvantages. The crucial factor in a child's successful development is not how many children are in the family, but how the child and his or her parents relate. If the relationship is unhealthy—if parents expect too much or the child demands too much, for example—the child is likely to be poorly adjusted. However, if the relationship is warm and balanced, the child's personality and behavior will reflect that quality.

Earlier in this chapter, two "popular" stereotypes of single children were described. It is likely that you thought of at least one single child who fit the spoiled brat description and perhaps another who could be described as a shrinking violet. Now, think beyond the first one or two single children who came to your mind and list all the single children you know. Reflect on those individuals and assess how nearly each fits the traditional views of single children.

Chances are that your list will be longer than you would have guessed. It is also likely that your list will contain the names of some people you admire and some you don't. Look carefully at the balance. Is the ratio about what you would expect in any cross section of acquaintances? Think about the individual family situations of the people on your list. Do you think their family situations were important in the kind of person each became? Do you think the single children on your list would have been different if they had had siblings?

Being the only child is an important factor in the life of a single child—but it is not the only factor. It probably is not even the most important factor.

As for the question, "Is being a single child fair to the child?"—the answer is "Yes!"

three / *Having One Child – Is It Fair to the Parents?*

Parents of an only child put all their eggs in one basket.

A Parent of Two Children

In his book *Family Constellation*, Walter Toman concludes a chapter on single children with this statement: "Under all circumstances. . . one should ask the question why there has been only one child. What was *wrong* with the parents?" (italics ours)[1]

Like Toman, many people in American society are critical of parents who have one child. Fifty-five percent of the one-child parents in our study said that they had been criticized for having a single child—or at least advised against the decision (Appendix 2). "I've had people I barely know ask why we have only one child," remarked Celeste, the mother of a five-year-old daughter. "Regardless of how I answer, they usually tell me what a big mistake we're making." Some of the specific comments other parents recalled were: "It's wrong for you to deny your child the fun of brothers and sisters," "You can't know the real joys of parenthood until you see your two children play together," and "You'll regret your decision in later years."

Underlying many of these comments is the suggestion that parents who have only one child are selfish. In failing to provide a sibling for their child, parents are thought to put parental interest above the well-being of their youngster. Daniel, the father of a teen-ager, remarked, "Our sixteen-year-old son is a healthy, popular, well-adjusted young man. But my mother still tells me that my wife and I are selfish not to have another child." While a single child is seen as the "victim" of onliness, his or her parents are held responsible for the condition.

Is the criticism of one-child parents justified? In this chapter we examine research on parents of single children and explore what parents say about themselves and their family experiences. Our attempt is to discover what, *if anything*, is wrong with parents of one child.

One-Child Parents—What Are They Like?

Some parents want to have a single child, but others do so by default. Both types of parents were represented in our study. Parents who chose to have a single child made their decision for a variety of reasons—to devote more time to their careers, to avoid another two years of infancy, to demonstrate their concern for overpopulation, to devote more time to their marriage, and/or to save money. However, these parents clearly stated that they had made a conscious decision to have, or remain, a single-child family.

Other one-child parents did not purposely decide to have a single child. Some were divorced or widowed after having one child and did not remarry, or remarried and the new spouse did not want another child. Others attributed their one-child family to health restrictions or "uncontrollable circumstances." As one mother said, "God just didn't give us any more." Although it might be argued that these parents could have changed their situation by adopting a child, they view their one-child family as happenstance. They are not necessarily unhappy with their family size, but they do not regard it as "planned."

In describing the characteristics of one-child parents, we refer primarily to parents who make a decision to have a single child. However, these characteristics also seem typical of parents who have a single child by default.

Family Background

"I was one of thirteen children," explained Earl, the father of a single child, "and I was determined to have only one child of my own. I wanted to be able to give that child all the attention and things I missed when I was growing up."

Studies show that some people, like Earl, are influenced by their own family experiences in deciding how many children to have.[2] In analyzing the family size of one-child parents in our study, we found an unusually large proportion of mothers—40 per cent—had grown up in large families (five or more children). The percentage of fathers from large families (23 per cent) was smaller, but still high (Appendix 2). In interviews, several parents specifically stated that their experience growing up with many brothers and sisters had influenced them to have one child. For instance, Faye, the eldest daughter in a family of seven, made it clear that her one-child decision resulted from her childhood experience.

"As oldest daughter in such a big family," Faye explained, "I took care of so many kids that by the time I was fifteen I didn't care if I ever saw another one. When I married at age thirty-two—very late in my generation—I told my husband I only wanted one child. He was from a big family too, so it was okay with him."

We asked the one-child parents who had siblings if they had been "close" to their brothers and sisters as children and as adults. The answer was a definite "yes," especially for mothers. Ninety per cent of the mothers considered themselves close to siblings in both childhood and adulthood. Fewer fathers considered themselves close (83 per cent in childhood and 69 per cent in adulthood), but still the large majority had good relationships with their siblings (Appendix 2). The responses of these parents indicate that having a "close" relationship with brothers and sisters does not necessarily sway parents to have more than one child of their own.

Among the one-child parents in our study was also a relatively high percentage who had no siblings. Eighteen per cent of the fathers and 10 per cent of the mothers were single children themselves (Appendix 2). Some told us they had chosen to have one child because of their own childhood experiences. "I had a very happy childhood," said Jo Ellen, a single child, "and I wanted to provide the same kind of experience for my son. Besides I don't know if I would be comfortable trying to deal with more than one child."

Marriage/Parenting Patterns

When Norma Cutts and Nicholas Moseley conducted their study of single children in the 1950s, they found that 53 per cent of their subjects had been born to parents over age 30.[3] In that year the average American mother bore her last child by age 27. Cutts and Moseley concluded that one-child parents tend to be older when their child is born than multichild parents are when their first child is born.[4]

The background information on the one-child parents in our study revealed that they too tended to be older than the average parent when their child was born. The typical American woman now has her first child at age 22,[5] but 83 per cent of the mothers in our study were past age 23 when their child was born. More than one-third were 30 or older. The fathers reflected a similar age pattern. Eighty per cent were past age 24 when their child was born; 36 per cent were past 30 (Appendix 2).

In addition to being older at the birth of their child, parents of single children also tend to have been married longer than the average couple when they become parents. The average length of time between an American couple's marriage and the birth of their first child is two years.[6] Sixty-four per cent of the couples in our study had been married three years or longer when their child was born or adopted (Appendix 2). "Difficulty in getting pregnant" was the reason parents gave most frequently for not having their child earlier.

Since one-child parents tend to be older and to introduce a child into their marriage later than other couples, how does their marital adjustment and satisfaction compare with that of multichild parents? Unfortunately most of the research on this question was done a number of years ago. A Milbank Memorial Fund study found that more one-child parents rated their marriage "happy" than any other group of parents and that marital happiness decreased with each additional child.[7] Burgess and Cottrell found couples with one child had better marital adjustment scores than couples with more children.[8] In a study of 22,000 couples, R.O. Lang concluded that among the couples married longer than five years, those with one or two children had significantly better adjustment scores than those with no children or more than two children, but he did not distinguish between one- and two-child parents.[9]

In a more recent study on marriage and children, Robert Blood and Donald Wolfe reached a different conclusion than the earlier researchers. They found that the marital satisfaction of couples with one and two children was somewhat less than couples with three children.[10] Divorce statistics also have been cited by some critics as evidence that one-child parents have poorer marital adjustment than other parents. In 1970 the U.S. Census Bureau compiled reports from 16 states, which showed that 41 per cent of all divorces involving children were granted to parents with one child.[11] On the basis of this rather high percentage, it has been suggested that having just one child causes more marital problems and subsequent divorces than having more. But the interpretation is misleading. It is more likely that one-child parents who divorce limited their family to one because they were unhappy—not because having one child made them unhappy. This was the case with Rhoda.

"Our marriage started falling apart after the first month," stated Rhoda in an interview, "but we decided to try the old strategy of having a child to hold our marriage together. It didn't work. Although we both loved the child, she didn't do a thing for our relationship, and we vowed not to complicate things with another child. When our daughter was four we separated, happy to have one child, but glad not to have more children to worry about."

Personalities

Choosing to have one child is an atypical (and often unpopular) choice in our society. Are the personalities of parents who make this choice different from multichild parents? Although no research has been conducted on the personalities of one-child fathers, one study shows that one-child mothers tend to have stronger career and personal interests than multichild mothers. Eleanor Lewis, who conducted this study, concluded that the one-child mother is "less dependent on traditional forms of self-esteem and more independent than traditionally reared women."[12]

Being "nontraditional" does not seem to affect the one-child mother's satisfaction with her role as mother. Ivan Nye found that mothers with one child are more content with their mothering role than mothers of any other number of children.[13] A one-child mother and nursing instructor we interviewed commented, "Although I get constant pressure from family and friends to have a second child, I feel I have the best of both worlds with an only. I can express my maternal instincts and still have enough time to be successful in my career."

As a group, the one-child parents we interviewed seemed more adult-oriented than child-oriented. Both mothers and fathers made frequent references to their careers and outside activities or hobbies. Although their child was an important part of their lives, many parents clearly had other interests and were not "living through their child." The adult orientation of one-child parents may well result from being older when their child is born. A person who is 25 or 30 before becoming a parent has had more time to establish adult interests and a career than a person who becomes a parent at age 20.

The characteristics of one-child parents we have described are generalizations. They do not describe every parent of a single child; nor does every parent exhibit each characteristic. However, the tendency for one-child parents to be older and have somewhat nontraditional personalities may influence their perceptions of the pros and cons of the one-child family.

Having a Single Child: The Disadvantages

In our study we asked one-child parents if they thought there were advantages in having one child. Seventy-nine per cent said "yes." Then we asked if they thought there were problems. This time a smaller, but still significant, proportion (65 per cent) replied "yes" (Appendix 2). To answer the question, "Is it fair to parents to have a single child?" the parents' explanations of both the advantages and problems in parenting one child are important. Consider first the disadvantages discussed by parents.

Always a First-Time Parent

"My biggest problem in growing up," remarked an adult only, "was not being an *only* child—it was being a *first* child.

My parents were always practicing on me." This statement points out one of the crucial facts about parenting a single child—parents of one child are forever first-time parents. Some research suggests that parents behave differently toward their first child than toward their subsequent children.

In a study of 46 couples having more than one child, Joan Lasko observed that the parents were more restrictive and less warm toward the first child than toward subsequent children.[14] This finding runs contrary to the common belief that parents spoil and overindulge their first child. When parents in another study were asked, "Did you change your methods of handling children between the first and second child?" 65 per cent replied that they had "relaxed more" with their second, while only three per cent felt they had become "stricter."[15] The pressure's off with your second child," remarked a father of two sons. "You've already proved yourself as a parent with the first child, so you can sit back and enjoy the second one."

For one-child parents, the pressure is never off. Whether they respond by being more restrictive or more indulgent than other parents, they are not likely to be as relaxed as parents who have several children.

Death of a Single Child

Always being a first-time parent is a minor disadvantage when compared to the possibility of having a single child die. When Milbank Memorial Fund researchers asked couples what influenced them to have a second child, 33 per cent of the wives and 23 per cent of the husbands reported that they were "very much influenced" in their decision by the thought of being left childless if their first child should die.[16] All parents, regardless of how many children they have, face the potential of some tragedy leaving them childless, but the likelihood is, of course, greater for parents who have only one child. One-child parents readily acknowledge that the fear of their child's death is a concern they must come to terms with.

In discussing the problems they had confronted in raising their daughter, one couple said the thought of losing their single child had been very distressing to them for several years. "We finally realized," explained the mother, "that our concern about losing our daughter was legitimate, but that having a second child would not solve the problem. If we should lose our daughter, another child could not replace her. People who believe that one child can take the place of another do not value individual life very highly. Human beings are not replaceable parts."

Not only do parents of onlies think about the eventuality of their child's death, but other people draw their attention to the possibility. One parent said she remembered several instances when acquaintances had asked, "What if Kevin should be taken from you (die)?" When we asked how she responded, the mother replied, "I'd just tell them I would be grateful for the time we had him, and I was sure he would make a lovely angel."

The death of any child is a tragedy for parents. The parents of single children run the risk of being left childless if their son or daughter dies, but the loss of their child is certainly no more profound for them than such a death is for any other parent.

Parents Must Be the Child's Playmate

"The best thing about having two kids is that they entertain each other," remarked a mother as she watched her children play frisbee. Who entertains the single child? Apparently parents often fill their single child's need for companionship. One-child parents in our study said that at each stage of their child's development they had spent more time with their child (or spent more time arranging for companions) than they would have if there had been more children in the family (Appendix 2).

The crucial question is not how much time one-child parents spend with their child, but how they feel about spending that time. The parents we surveyed had mixed emotions. In discussing advantages of raising a single child, the parents' second most frequent response was "being able to provide that child lots of time and attention." However, they also viewed companionship as a problem. Statements such as "parents have to be companions" and "the child expects (gets) too much parent attention" were the most often mentioned disadvantages of rearing one child (Appendix 2).

The saving grace in this dilemma is that the adultlike behavior and interests of single children make it attractive for parents to be their companions. The single child tends to adopt the interests and mannerisms of the parents and "fits" more easily into adult activities than several children do. One parent said, "We made a miniature adult of our son. Our friends accused us of not letting him be a child, and maybe we did overdo it. But in the long run it was an advantage to Alex and to us. How many parents can take a six-year-old to Europe for two months and all three of them enjoy it?"

For adults who enjoy providing companionship to a child, the single child's need for parental companionship may not seem a disadvantage. For parents who do not relish a child's constant company, the child's need for companionship can be a problem.

Parents Often Overexpect, Overprotect

"You put a lot of pressure on the child when you've got just one," remarked a middle-aged father. "You've got no margin of error." His statement emphasizes a common feeling among one-child parents that they tend to have higher expectations for their child than other parents. Because of their high expectations, one-child parents often plead guilty to pressuring their son or daughter to succeed.

In a study of parent/child interaction, Irma Hilton found that mothers of one young child behaved differently with their child than mothers with more children. Dr. Hilton took each child and its mother into a room where the child was given a series of puzzles to complete while the mother was instructed to unobstrusively observe her child. After five minutes the testing was interrupted, and the mother was told that her child was not doing as well as other children had done. Then the mother was observed interacting with her child for another five-minute period. Observers noted that the one-child mothers more often interfered with and directed their child's activity than the multichild mothers.[17] These tendencies often continue throughout the life of a single child.

Many parents recognize their tendencies to both push and shelter their children more than parents with larger families. Twenty-eight per cent of the disadvantages named by one-child parents in our study related to the tendency of parents to overexpect and/or overprotect their single child (Appendix 2). "I desperately want my child to do well in life," commented a one-child mother of a teen-age daughter. "Since I've got only one, I push her to make straight A's, be the president of her senior class, and go to law school. At the same time I try to baby her. I feel uneasy when she goes out on dates or when she goes out of town on a school activity. I have a great urge to try to protect her from everything I feel might be difficult or negative."

Social Criticism and Pressure

"My husband and I were married for ten years before our child was born," reported Diane, the mother of a first-grade child. "For seven of those years many of our friends and relatives nagged us with the question, 'When are you going to have children?'

"When our child was born," Diane continued, "we

breathed a sigh of relief and said, 'Well, at least they'll get off our backs now.' But we were wrong. After about two years we began to hear, 'When are you going to get Jimmy a little brother or sister?' Jimmy is now six, and the questions haven't stopped yet. In fact, I think there's more pressure to have a second child than there was to have the first."

More than half (56 per cent) of the parents we interviewed stated that they had been criticized, either mildly or severely, about their decision to have one child (Appendix 2). Some of the comments reported by parents were:

> It's not fair to the child.
> Your child will be lonely.
> Your child will be spoiled.
> What'll you do when he/she leaves?
> You're being selfish.
> What if something happens to your child?
> Two children are no harder to raise than one.
> Your child is missing 'something.'
> It's a shame.
> It's not normal.

Most parents felt that pressure from their own parents was the most difficult to ignore. "I know it's really none of their business, but when my parents start talking about how they would like to have more grandchildren, I take it more seriously than when other people talk about the 'mistake' we're making," one young mother remarked.

Some parents feel the social pressure to have a second child is an important disadvantage of the one-child family. Others consider such pressure just a nuisance. Like the other disadvantages of having a single child, it is a consequence which must be weighed against the advantages of the one-child family.

Having a Single Child: The Advantages

When one-child parents in our study discussed the disadvantages of having one child, they tended to name similar problems. However, when they discussed the advantages of the one-child family, their answers were much more diverse and personal. Among the varied responses, seven were most prominent.

Financial

"Raising one kid is cheaper than raising two," said the father of a single child when asked to name the advantages of having one child. Many one-child parents agree. "Costs less" was the advantage those in our study most often named (Appendix 2).

The parents' observation is not a minor point. In 1969 the U.S. Commission on Population Growth and the American Future estimated the basic cost of rearing a child from birth through college to be over $40,000. By 1976, inflation pushed that figure to at least $53,000. The cost can run to as much as $133,000 if the mother quits her job to stay home with the child for a few years. Contrary to the "cheaper by the dozen" theory, rearing does not get less expensive after the first child; the Commission estimated that it costs only about $500 less to rear a second or subsequent child.[18]

Restricting child-rearing expense is important to some parents because it puts less pressure on the family bread winner (or winners) to produce an adequate income. "We have an only child because my husband is starting his own electronics business and things are tight financially," explained one mother. For other parents, having one child simply means there is more money in the family budget to pursue the interests of all family members. "Frankly, we enjoy having more money to spend on ourselves," said a one-child father. "If they invent a cost-free child, we might consider having another. But until then we'll stick with one."

More Time to Enjoy the Child

"I've always felt the real advantage of having only one child is that I have time to stop and enjoy my daughter," remarked the mother of a teenager. "With no other child to demand my attention, I can quit whatever I'm doing and talk to Kathleen when the opportunity or need arises. Mothers who have other children to attend can't always take that kind of time for each child. It seems like they always end up 'oiling the squeaky wheel.' "

Like single children, one-child parents believe their family size promotes good parent-child communication and interaction. Statements such as "having more time to enjoy my child" accounted for approximately one-fourth of the benefits mentioned by one-child parents in our survey (Appendix 2).

How one-child families use their time depends on the personalities and interests of both parents and child, although the interests of parents probably set the tone for family activities. The Hillman family illustrates one life-style. Mrs. Hillman is a trained pianist, Mr. Hillman, a violinist, and their daughter, Eunice, a talented clarinetist. "Some of our fondest memories are of the evenings we spent playing as a trio while Eunice was growing up," recalls Mrs. Hillman. "None of us is particularly outgoing, and a great deal of our family life revolved around making lovely music in our living room."

Another mother described a quite different life-style. "We have a boat we use all summer to water ski and fish. When the snow flies, we put away the boat, get out our snow skis, and head for the mountains. We might lead the same kind of life if we had more children, but I doubt if we would have the time or the money."

Freedom from Favoritism

A problem completely avoided in the one-child family is concern by parents that they may be favoring one child over others. "I've tried to be fair to each of my kids," complained a father of three, "but despite my efforts the two youngest have always felt I favored Tony, my oldest. At this moment they're not speaking to me, or him, because I loaned him the money to start his own business and didn't give them an equal amount."

Parents with several children seldom acknowledge that they have a favorite among their offspring, but their actions often show distinct preferences. When we asked college students with siblings "Do you think you received more attention from your parents than did your brothers and sisters?" 25 per cent said "yes" (Appendix 5). Dr. Elizabeth Hurlock writes, "Parents react differently to different children, and they show it by their attitudes and actions. In spite of the typical parent's claim that he 'loves all his children equally,' his actions are not so convincing to his children."[19]

Closer Relationship with Child

In discussing their one-child family, the Kellys said they felt that their relationship with their child was closer than most parent/child relationships in multichild families. "It's hard to explain," observed Mrs. Kelly, "but the bond between Kevin and us seems stronger than between parents and children in larger families." During a separate interview, Kevin commented that he felt he had a closer relationship with his parents than most of his friends had with their parents. "I'm not saying we get along better," he said, "because my folks and I really have big arguments at times. But we feel close. Maybe it's because they've always kind of treated me like an adult—like one of them rather than like a kid."

Other single children and their parents agree with the Kelly family. In describing their parent-child relationship, parents suggested some reasons for the family closeness they felt:

> Our child became part of our adult world, and we were a three-adult family rather than a family in which children stand apart from parents.
>
> We viewed ourselves as three against the world, and that united us.
>
> Our family was small so we spent what time we had with each other.
>
> Our interests were alike and the three of us did many things together.

The bond between parents and their single child may grow stronger because they tend to have more similar attitudes and values than parents and children in larger families. Bernard Rosen found single children and oldest children had values about achievement more similar to those of their mothers than did youngest or middle-born children.[20] "Our son is certainly not a carbon copy of us," remarked a one-child father, "but he shares most of our views on politics, religion, and the like. Maybe it's because we always took a lot of time to explain our beliefs to him."

Although not all parents develop a close relationship with their single child, many one-child parents feel that their parent/child relationship is better than average. "There are lots of problems parenting an only child," remarked one mother, "but they're all surpassed by the special closeness we have with our daughter."

More Time for Careers

"My husband and I have owned and run this hardware store for twenty-five years," explained the mother of an adult daughter. "Sharon slept in a crib behind the saw blades when she was a baby and learned to ride her tricycle in the aisles. We used to joke about her cutting teeth on tenpenny nails. By having just one child, my husband and I were able to continue working together. If I'd had more kids I probably wouldn't have been able to stay active in the business."

Careers and parenting seem easier to combine in one-child families. For the father, having one rather than several children eases both the financial and time pressures of parenting, but the mother's career is more significantly affected by the number of children in the family.

Research shows that one-child mothers are more likely to work outside the home than multichild mothers.[21] One explanation is that one-child mothers limit their family size so they can more easily pursue careers. Another explanation is that one-child mothers take jobs because parenting one youngster is not sufficiently engrossing to maintain their interest in exclusive homemaking. Whatever their reason for working outside the home, many one-child mothers believe the combination of career and parenting is ideal. Betty, a fashion merchandiser who has a teen-age son, is such a mother. "I really enjoy working," said Betty, "but I also think it's imperative that I have a career. I'm afraid if I stayed home I'd drive myself (and my child) crazy. By working I'm busy enough that I don't have time to tie him to my apron strings."

Not all mothers of single children need or want to work. However, those who do may find the demands of job and home easier to meet with one child. "It's simple arithmetic," in the opinion of one mother of a three-year-old. "I devote ten hours a day to my job and commuting. I give my child approximately four hours of fairly undivided time when I'm at home. Providing I sleep eight hours, that leaves about two hours for my husband and myself. Another child could easily consume those two hours. I'm just not willing to give them up."

More Time for Spouse

"I believe the roles of wife and mother are basically incompatible," explained a one-child mother. "At least I can't handle both comfortably. Time is the problem. Mothering cuts into my time with my husband dramatically. Since I was a wife first and hope to be a wife long after my mothering duties are done, I decided not to interrupt my marriage relationship with more than one child."

Although not all couples feel that a child strains their marital relationship, some do. Eleanor Lewis found couples who voluntarily had one child reported that intimacy was an important part of their relationship and that the husband enjoyed being nurtured by his wife. She concluded that their need for intimacy may have been the reason these couples chose to have only one child.[22]

The nurture of a marriage and the nurture of children are both demanding tasks. Because rearing one child requires less time and energy than rearing more children, one-child parents have more opportunity to engage in communication and activities which will strengthen their marriage. For couples whose relationship thrives on one-to-one communication, touching, and shared interests, having one child may be more compatible with their marriage relationship than having several children.

An Orderly Household

One-child parents have a unique opportunity to experience the joys of parenting without having to tolerate the household "noise and commotion" created by two or more children. "The part I like best about the one-child family," said the mother of an eight-year-old, "is having some semblance of sanity in this household. Jeff often brings his neighborhood friends to our house to play. While I enjoy having them here, it's always a great relief when they leave and the house is quiet." Sixty-four per cent of the two-child mothers in our study felt that there was more noise in the household after their second entered the family unit (Appendix 4).

The degree of order and quiet in a one-child family is largely determined by the temperament of the parents. If parents place a high premium on orderliness, a single child is likely to adopt their view of the acceptable household noise level and procedure; two or more children are less likely to conform. The single child is less "kidlike" than a youngster whose siblings constantly reinforce childlike behavior.

People who are unruffled by noise and clutter will not consider orderliness a notable benefit of having one child. However, for the parent who values a relatively peaceful home atmosphere, it is a definite plus. This advantage combined with the others we've noted make the one-child family more attractive than its critics suggest.

One-Child Parents—Yesterday and Today

Important changes in family styles and personal values have made parenting today a different experience than it was some years ago. Our study included both parents whose child is now an adult and younger parents whose child is under age 18. We compared their responses on survey questions to determine if the attitudes and views of today's one-child parents are different from those of parents who reared their child one or more generations ago.

In general, the responses from the two groups were quite similar. The parents' ages, duration of marriage before having children, and family backgrounds did not show remarkable differences. Their reasons for having a single child were similar. They also closely agreed on the advantages and disadvantages of raising a single child. But one question did elicit an important difference.

In responding to the question, "Have there been people who expressed approval of your one-child family?", 50 per cent of the older parents replied "yes." Among the younger parents that percentage increased to 65 per cent (Appendix 2). Although the increase is not dramatic, it does suggest that parents who choose the one-child family today are finding more social approval than did their counterparts in years past. Parenting a single child has traditionally been regarded as "second-class" parenting, but the image may be improving.

Having One Child—Is It Fair to Parents?

Like every family size, the one-child family has certain inherent disadvantages for parents. The limited parental perspective, the companionship demands, and the prospect of being left childless are particularly troubling. However, nothing indicates there are more parental disadvantages in having one child than in having more children. Neither is there evidence that the disadvantages are *more serious* than those associated with other family sizes.

Balancing the problems of parenting one child are the advantages that one-child parents enjoy. Perhaps the most attractive aspect of having one child is that parents can experience the rewards and joys of parenting without drastically restricting their personal and marital interests. For many parents who choose to have one child, the family-style offers a happy compromise between no children and two children.

Is the one-child family fair to parents? For parents who carefully weigh the pros and cons of the one-child family and find that it offers what they want from parenting, the one-child life-style is not just fair—it is superior.

four / *One, Two, or More Children— What Are the Differences?*

One child is good. Two should be even better.

A MOTHER PREGNANT WITH
HER SECOND CHILD

"We were ambivalent for several years before we decided to have our first child," recalled Clarice, the mother of two sons. "We considered parenthood a profound decision and carefully weighed all the pros and cons. But the decision to have a second child was entirely different. We hardly gave it any thought at all. I guess we felt because we'd had one, we automatically had to have a second."

Why do 90 per cent of all parents have or expect to have a second child rather than stop with one?[1] Is the decision as "automatic" as Clarice suggests? To find out, we asked 245 mothers of two children when and why they decided to have a second child (Appendix 4).

Forty-three per cent of the mothers said that they made the decision to have a second child before their first was born. Although these mothers may have carefully pondered the question of whether to have *any* children, when they decided to become parents they also decided to have at least two children. Remembering her experience, one mother said, "Once we decided to take the parenthood trip, we talked only in terms of two children. I don't think either of us considered stopping with one."

As to why they decided to have a second child, the largest number of mothers (45 per cent) said that raising their first child had been a rewarding experience and they wanted to repeat it. Other mothers (29 per cent) said they had a second child to "provide a companion for their first child." Some of these mothers said that they felt a single child would be "lonely" or "handicapped." Others said that although they did not personally believe the "only child tales," they had been convinced by relatives or friends to have a second child "for the good of their first."

Eight per cent of the mothers felt they needed more than one child to be fulfilled in their mothering role. "I just didn't feel like a 'real' mother with only one child," wrote one mother. Another eight per cent reported that they had a second child "because my husband wanted it." For still others, the sex of their first child was a consideration. Six per cent of the mothers said that because their first child was a girl, they decided to try again for a boy.

In general, the mothers in our study believed that having a second child would bring benefits to them as parents and to their first child. Did the benefits follow? Do additional children really "double your pleasure and double your fun?" In this chapter we will explore the effect of adding a second, third, and subsequent children to the one-child family.

No Two Children Are Alike

Teresa is a mother of two daughters, ages four and seven. For her, parenthood has been full of surprises.

> My first daughter is a *"Ladies Home Journal* child" if there ever was one. She's beautiful, charming, bright, and well behaved. Naturally I

was eager to have a second child. I envisioned basically a carbon copy of my first—with a few modifications in appearance, personality, and maybe sex.

What a shock my second daughter was. Instead of being a pleasant, quiet child, she's rowdy, demanding, and strong-willed. Raising her is not an experience—it's a trial. I can't understand how two kids—both mine—can be so different.

Not long after the birth or adoption of a new child, many parents make an important discovery—their new child is different (often radically different) from their first child. A common expression among the two-child mothers in our study was "my second child was amazingly different from my first." "From the moment we got home from the hospital," said one mother, "I knew 'number two son' wasn't going to be a repeat of 'number one son.'"

For parents, the realization that their second child is not going to be a carbon copy of their first is perplexing. Like Teresa, these parents find it hard to believe that their children are so different. "After all, they have the same parents, live in the same house, and share the same experiences," mused one father. "How can they react so differently?"

Although it is true that siblings grow up in the same household and have the same parents, they never have identical circumstances or experiences. Several conditions are likely to produce siblings "as different as night and day."

Genetic Differences

Differences in children begin with the special genetic makeup of each child. The unique fusing of the parents' male and female chromosomes determines the sex, size, appearance, intelligence, and innate abilities of their offspring. From the moment of conception, children are destined to be different, not similar.

Birth Position

For some 20 years, Dr. Lucille Forer, a clinical psychologist, has examined the effects of "birth order" on personality. She concludes that a person's birth position in the family greatly influences the kind of personality he or she develops. First-borns, for example, tend to be conscientious, achieving, and approval-seeking, but they are also jealous and tense. In contrast, middle-borns are likely to be diplomatic and vigorous, but attention-seeking and undependable. Last-borns generally are charming, playful, and lighthearted, but more spoiled, irresponsible, and less achievement-oriented than older siblings.[2]

The effects of being oldest, middle, or youngest are complicated by the number of years between the siblings. When children are widely spaced (more than four years apart), their interests and abilities are vastly different, and they generally have little to do with each other. Their personality development is less influenced by their sibling(s) and more influenced by their parents. In contrast, when siblings are close in age, they tend to be very companionable and highly influenced by each other. But the close spacing sets up a highly competitive situation, which often turns siblings into jealous rivals.

Whether siblings are boys or girls also makes a difference in personality development. After studying the effects of sex patterns, Dr. Helen Koch concluded that siblings of the same sex tend to identify more closely with each other than siblings of opposite sexes. However, she believes opposite sex pairs are more stimulating to each other and develop more curiosity, enthusiasm, ambition, and tenacity than children having siblings of the same sex.[3]

Although siblings are members of the same family, they do

not have identical "status" in the family. Siblings' family position, age, and sex destine each child to play a different role in the family and to develop a unique set of needs and behaviors.

Parents

Despite parents' frequent declaration that they treat all their children alike, the interaction between parents and each child is different. Often the tone of the parent/child relationship is set by the parents' attitude about the child's birth. First-time parents who have eagerly awaited the arrival of their child respond differently to that child than to a fourth, unplanned child. "Everything is an adventure with your first child—even getting up in the middle of the night," said the mother of three. "With later children, those 'adventures' become 'chores.'"

The age of parents is also important. Twenty-year-old mothers and fathers typically respond to their children with more energy than 40-year-old parents. But the life experiences of older parents may help them relate to their child in a less anxious way than young parents.

One of the most important components of the parent/child relationship is difficult to measure. Between parent and child, as between all other individuals, there is an intangible "chemistry." The personality chemistry is sometimes "right" with a parent and one child, but "wrong" with another child. "I love both my sons," said one father in a candid moment, "but I like one better than the other."

Family Circumstances

In addition to the influences of siblings and parents, a child is molded by other, more general family circumstances. The parents' separation or divorce, for example, will affect each child's development differently. The critical or prolonged illness of a family member, either parent or child, will have its effect. And stepbrothers, stepsisters, adopted children, grandparents, or other relatives living in the household will influence the formation of different personalities.

The family's economic situation is also important, particularly when it changes significantly over time. "My parents were struggling to keep their small farm intact most of my childhood, and there were times we barely had enough to eat," recalls the oldest of five children. "By the time my youngest sister was born (eighteen years later), my parents were turning a good profit. Her childhood experiences and mine were so opposite it's like we grew up in two different families."

Genetic makeup, birth order, age of parents, the presence or absence of others in the household, and the financial status of the family help insure that each child in a family will be different. Parents who decide to have another child because they want a repeat performance of their "dream" child should realize that subsequent children may be quite different. Instead of being a repeat performance, each child will be a brand new show.

The Two-Child Family

At this time in the United States, the two-child family is the most popular family size—35 per cent of all parents have or expect to have two children.[4] Even more think two is the "ideal" family size. Three national surveys show about 50 per cent of young American couples believe a two-child family is best.[5] Is this family size as ideal as its advocates suggest?

Children in a Two-Child Family

Being one of two children in a family has predictable consequences for each child—but the consequences for the older child are very different than those for the younger child.

"I was an only child for seven years," recalls Charon, the older of two daughters. "I desperately wanted a little sister and badgered my mother constantly to have a baby. Well, she did, and I couldn't have been more surprised—or disappointed. Rather than being a playmate as I'd thought a sister would be, she was a helpless, colicky, demanding infant. Not only was she no fun, she deprived me of the undivided attention my mother had always given me. I suppose it was largely my early resentment that kept us from ever establishing a close relationship."

As Charon suggests, the older child in a two-child family is for a time a single child. As a single child, the youngster derives all the benefits of onliness—undivided parental attention, an uncompetitive atmosphere, unrestricted experiences and opportunities. When the second child arrives, a crisis occurs for the first child, who is "dethroned" from his or her unique position. Even if the first child has expressed a great desire for a brother or sister, the sibling soon becomes a rival for parent's attention and a threat to the firstborn's life-style.

An older child typically responds to the second's challenge by intensifying efforts to please his or her parents. Various studies demonstrate that firstborns are higher than later-borns in intellectual achievement, motivation, respect for authority, and conformity.[6] But studies also indicate that older children tend to be more anxious, jealous, angry, and unhappy—perhaps because they never quite recover from the dethronement shock.[7]

The experience of the younger child stands in contrast to his or her older sibling. Although the younger child never enjoys the pleasures of being a single child, he or she never suffers the anxiety of being challenged by a younger child According to Dr. Forer, "the younger boy or girl becomes the parents' favorite, because he or she adopts different tactics from the more demanding older child."[8] For example, if his or her older sibling pleases parents by excelling in school work, the younger child may attempt to gain parents' favor by being more openly affectionate or identifying more with parents' interests. "My older sister was a brain," commented Sue, the younger of two daughters. "I knew very early that I couldn't compete intellectually with her, so I decided to be more popular than she was. My parents were as pleased about my being homecoming queen as my sister winning a college scholarship."

Although a second child enjoys some advantages, there is one disadvantage to be reckoned with—a younger child is in constant competition with his or her older sibling and is almost always second best (at least in childhood). "I was a good athlete," recalls a college student who is the younger of two brothers. "But as good as I was, I could never beat my brother, who is three years older, in a race or wrestling match. It really bothered me to always lose to him even though I could do well against children my own age." The younger child's "second best" experiences at home may help to account for research findings showing later-born children to be less achievement-oriented than firstborns.[9]

Parents in a Two-Child Family

Adding a second child to the family unit affects not just the children—it affects the parents' experience as well. A story is told of a firstborn who swallowed a quarter. The child's parents, typically anxious, rushed the child to the hospital and had his stomach pumped. Some years later their second child swallowed a quarter. This time the more experienced parents simply looked at the child and said, "That will come out of your allowance."

We asked the mothers of two children in our survey what differences they noticed between having one and two children. Although these mothers generally felt positive about their decision to have a second child, they acknowledged that some significant changes in their household occurred when their second child was born or adopted (Appendix 4).

More Noise

One difference many mothers notice between one and two children is an increase in the household noise level. "Rather than playing quietly with each other, my kids fight," reflected a mother of two. "Their bickering really unnerves me. The thing I miss about having an only child is peace and quiet." Seventy-eight per cent of the mothers we surveyed agreed that two children created more noise than one. Three per cent thought there was less noise.

Less Time for Myself

Other mothers believe the biggest difference in having one and having two is time. Sixty-one per cent of the mothers reported having "less time for myself" after their second child was born. One mother described her day as "totally absorbed" with responding to the varied needs of her two children.

"I thought I was deprived of time for reading and tennis when I just had Bobby," wrote this mother, "but I was still able to squeeze out a little time for myself. Since my second child was born two years ago, I've started four books and haven't finished any of them. As for tennis, I couldn't even tell you where my racket is."

More Work

Related to having less personal time is an increase in the amount of work involved in child-rearing. "Before my second child was born, I'd convinced myself that two children really wouldn't be. much more work than one," said one mother. "What a joke. Two are exactly twice as much work as one."

Although only 22 per cent of the reporting mothers felt that their work load had "doubled" with the second child, 70 per cent indicated that their work load had "increased." Only six per cent reported that "two children are as easy as one." "It's not the laundry or preparing more food that gets you," declared the mother of two school-age children. "It's taking two kids to the doctor, shopping for two, and providing 'stimulating experiences' for both of them—that's the real difference."

The differences in children's personalities seem to put special demands on parents. The mothers in our study frequently mentioned that trying to meet the different needs of two children had complicated parenting for them. "Because my children have different personalities, interests, and needs, I have to constantly adjust to make sure that each of them gets what he or she needs," remarked Fran, a mother of two. "For example, one of my sons wants me to stay with him until he goes to sleep, while the other one wants me to leave him alone. It's a constant juggling act, which increases the work and pressure of parenting for me."

More Joy

Despite their reports of increased noise, responsibility, and work, the majority of the mothers in our survey indicated that having a second child had increased their parenting joy. Some said they thought providing a companion for their first child was important, and they felt good that their children would have the sibling experience. Others said they were personally relieved not to have to worry about raising an "only child." And the mothers whose children were opposite in sex were delighted with their boy-girl family. In general, the mothers seemed to feel that having a second child had met their parenting goals and made the extra effort of another child worthwhile.

The Two-Child Family–An Ideal?

Is the two-child family the ideal family size? It does have some specific advantages. It's a small family, which allows members time and energy to pursue individual interests. Although two children strain the family budget more than one child, most parents can manage the cost of a second child without undue hardship. The children provide companionship for each other and keep parent's attention from getting too intense. By having two children, parents avoid the nemesis of having an "only child."

But the two-child family has some drawbacks—some serious ones. For the children, the two-child family is an intensely competitive family size. Whereas the single child has no competitor, the child with one sibling has a constant competitor. Comparisons between the children seem inevitable, and rivalry is common. The effects of such rivalry are reflected in the findings of studies, which show that children who have one (and in some instances two) siblings tend to be more jealous than other children.[10] The child with one sibling gains a companion, but the advantage of companionship is often outstripped by the pressure to compete.

For parents of two children, the problem of parental favoritism is serious, perhaps more than in other family sizes. When there are three or more siblings in the family, the children seem to accept the differential treatment more easily (if one child gets an extra present at Christmas, at least there are two others who don't). In the two-child family it is difficult for parents to convince one child that special attention to his or her sibling is not a direct threat that requires the parent to make immediate amends. "My two kids keep a constant scorecard," said a two-child mother. "If I don't do everything exactly the same for the two of them, they accuse me of playing favorites. It becomes pretty nasty at times."

Having a second child avoids some of the problems of larger and smaller families. But it creates other problems. The two-child family is not the "perfect" family size our society has claimed it to be.

The Three-Child Family

Although the three-child family is not as popular as the two-child, about 23 per cent of young married couples say that they expect to have three children.[11] The Frederick Manski family is a three-child family. "We had a third child because our first two were girls and we wanted a boy," reports Betty Manski. Gilbert and Maria Lopez also have three children, but for a different reason. "We really wanted a large family, maybe six, but three are all we can afford," remarked Gilbert. Is the three-child family just an expanded version of the two-child family? A close look suggests that it is not.

Children in a Three-Child Family

The situation of the oldest child in a three-child family does not vary much from that of the elder in a two-child family. In a three-child family, the firstborn must deal with being dethroned a second time, but this dethronement is not as traumatic as the first. Although a third child further diverts the parents' attention, the oldest remains the most able sibling and often the recipient of the most opportunities.

The last child among three has not one but two older siblings to model. Since there are two older children, the youngest of three may feel less pressure to compete than the younger of two children. He or she also reaps the rewards of parents who have already earned their parenting "stripes" and can relax in their relations with this last child. The youngest child is likely to be less motivated than his or her older siblings and to be less skillful at leading people, but he or she is more likely to be successful at manipulating others.

"I didn't think I could compete intellectually with my two brothers for my parents' attention, so I got around them all by being cute," remembers the sister of two older brothers.

It is the middle child's position in the three-child family that is most precarious. Having neither the distinction of being oldest or youngest, the middle child, according to Dr. Forer, often grows up feeling neglected.[12]

Mike, the second son in a family of three boys, acknowledges some of the "middle child" feelings.

> I've always felt that I got screwed by being the middle child. I haven't always admitted it publicly, but I've always felt that way. And I think with some justification.
>
> For one thing, I was never really sure how I stood with my parents. They always made a big deal out of my oldest brother being their "firstborn," their "number one son." They also fussed over my youngest brother because he was their "baby." But they never said anything about my being their "in-between."
>
> I also think I got fewer goodies in childhood. For instance, I was the only kid in the family who never had a room to myself. My oldest brother had a separate room until I got old enough to share it with him. When he left, my younger brother moved in with me. But when I left home, my youngest brother got the room to himself. That may seem like a small point, but it sticks in my mind. I guess it comes down to the fact that a middle child doesn't have much status.

As a result of frustration with his or her family position, a middle child often develops an excitable, demanding, attention-getting, and undependable personality.[13] Findings from a study with young children demonstrate this. In this situation, second-borns in families of three showed the highest level of verbal aggression toward other children and required more attention from teachers than other children.[14] Although not every middle child develops these tendencies, the potential for special problems is high for the child in the middle.

Parents in a Three-Child Family

How does the parenting experience change when a third child is added to the family. Obviously the parents' time, energy, and resources are spread thinner by the additional child. Parents also may find more clearly drawn battle lines between parents and children when family conflicts arise. "When there are two kids, it's an even match," says the father of three sons, "but the scales begin to tip in the kids' favor when they outnumber you."

Perhaps the most difficult aspect of parenting three children is confronting and resolving the middle child's feelings. "I feel I spend half my time trying to compensate for my second daughter's belief that she's gotten the short end of the stick because she's the middle child," remarked a mother of three. "If I had it to do over again, I would avoid having three children just to keep from coping with the middle-child syndrome."

The Three-Child Family: More Than Two Plus One

The father who said, "After two children it doesn't make much difference how many you have," was wrong. Adding just one more child poses a whole new set of interrelationships, and problems, for a family. Granted, the three-child family is still relatively small, allowing its members individualization and independence while lessening the intense competition of the two-child family. But it creates the peculiar and precarious situation of the lone middle child. The precariousness affects not just the middle child. It also affects the oldest and youngest children as they relate to the middle child, and it affects the parents as they relate to all three children.

Like the two-child family, the three-child family solves some problems of smaller and larger family sizes, but it too creates new problems. The three-child family is not problem-free.

Four or More: The Walton Family Syndrome

Although economic and population considerations are stopping most couples from having large families today, there is still a certain nostalgia in America about the virtues of the large family. Whether it's the real-life Kennedys or the television-life Waltons, large families are presumed to develop the admirable qualities of cooperation, responsibility, and a sense of family spirit. However, in their study of 100 large families, Bossard and Boll found that our perceptions of large families are not all true.[15]

The Large Family: A Close-Up

In a large family, the sheer force of numbers is important. Time, resources, and energies must be stretched to accommodate all family members. Interrelationships become complicated.

Bossard and Boll found that values change as families get larger. Members of a small family value independence and personal development; large family members value (by necessity) cooperation, harmony, and sharing.[16] They also found that members of large families tend to be assigned, or fall into, roles. One child will be popular, another responsible, still others will be socially ambitious, studious, irresponsible, sickly, or spoiled.[17]

Once a role is assigned, it is difficult for the sibling to get out of that role. "As oldest of five daughters," remarked a women now in her forties, "I was cast into the role of the responsible caretaker. My sisters still see me in that role, but frankly I'm tired of being responsible for them."

It is often claimed that a large family socializes children by teaching them how to interact and cope with a variety of individuals. But the large family may be less socializing than commonly thought. A study by Bernice Moore and Wayne Holtzman of 1,440 Texas high school students showed that large family youths felt more socially inadequate and alienated than children from smaller families.[18] By having so many built-in companions and family demands, the large family children tended to live within their families and to regard the rest of the world as foreign. One woman, a member of a six-child family, remembers her experience this way.

"My family was so close and got along so well that I never had any nonfamily friends when I was living at home. When I went away to college I had a terrible time adapting to living in the dorm because girls didn't seem to understand or accept me like my brothers and sisters had."

Parenting a large number of children is a completely different experience than parenting one, two, or three. Bossard and Boll contend that as each child is added, the interaction between parents and children decreases. Parenting becomes "extensive"; parents supervise and try to keep the whole ship sailing, but they interact only minimally with individual children. In the parents' place, older siblings take increased responsibility for the rearing of younger children, often to the point that the older children are exploited.[19] Lines of authority are more clearly drawn—they must be. The emphasis in a large family is not development but maintenance.

Large Families: How Desirable?

Just how nostalgic about large families should we be? Certainly there are admirable qualities about the "cheaper by the dozen" family type. Aside from developing coping mechanisms in its members, perhaps the greatest benefit of

the large family is the "sense of family" it develops among
family members. "Having so many kids in the family," recalled a woman with eight brothers and sisters, "was a financial nightmare for my parents, but there was security in our
numbers too. Home was a very poor place, but it was a warm
and reassuring place. The best friends I've got are my
brothers and sisters."

Interestingly, this same woman has chosen to have only
one child of her own. Apparently such a decision is not uncommon for people reared in large families. Bossard and
Boll found that the majority of siblings from large families
chose to have smaller than average families themselves, especially the eldest daughters who had been responsible for
much care of younger siblings.[20] The large family may present a sentimental picture-book image, but the experience is
not one that its members choose to repeat. "Any one who
says they want a large family should stop watching the Waltons and start looking at real families," said one man who
grew up with five siblings. "It's not all it's cracked up to be."

Making Family Size Decisions

In this chapter we have examined just what happens when a
family adds a second child, a third, or more. For parents, or
prospective parents, deciding how many children to have,
two implications are important.

First, there is no way that parents can predict what kind of
child they will have. It is impossible to guess accurately what a
first child will be like. It is equally impossible to predict what
a second or third or seventh will be like. Parents who have a
marvelous first parenting experience should recognize that
the second child may not be anything like that first child.
Each offspring is a new gamble. Those who think otherwise
need only to ask a few multichild parents to describe the
differences in their children.

Second, there is no such thing as an "ideal" family size.

Every family size has specific characteristics and involves specific advantages and disadvantages. The best family size for each couple depends on what advantages they want and what disadvantages they can tolerate.

It is especially important that parents deciding whether to have a second child recognize the special problems of the two-child family. Because there has been so much emphasis on the advantages of having two children, the disadvantages have been overlooked. The two-child family may eliminate concern about having a single child, but parents need to keep in mind the equally serious problem of competition in a two-child family unit.

Children do not come with a money-back guarantee. A second, or third, or fourth child can enhance parents' and children's family experiences. The child can also decrease satisfaction and adjustment. Having a second or subsequent child to assure family happiness is a risk.

five / *The Decision to Have One Child — a New Life-Style*

So the question is not how many children are right for a given family, but rather what kind of human beings that family can turn out.[1]

ALBERT ROSENFELD

"It was fairly easy for us to be intellectually convinced that having one child was a good idea," explained Suzette as she watched her lively two-year-old son. "Financially we knew it would be an advantage. It made sense from a population standpoint, and all the information we read assured us that an only child could be okay. But still we've had hesitations. It's not easy to set aside all the old wives' tales we've always heard about only children."

Suzette's statement relates directly to this book's central issue—making the decision to have a one-child family. Before you and your partner can confidently make a decision to have one child, two questions must be answered: 1) What personal consequences can you expect for yourselves and your child if you choose the one-child family life-style and 2) what consequences can society expect if more people choose to have one-child families? In this chapter we explore answers to these questions.

Personal Consequences of the One-Child Family

Every one-child family is unique. A one-child family in which the father is an astronaut is different from one in which the mother is a physician or the child a diabetic. Although these unique dimensions make it impossible to suggest precisely what the consequences of having a single child will be for each couple, certain general effects are predictable.

Planned Births

"My husband and I are great planners and organizers," reflected Lilly, the mother of one. "Naturally our decision to have a child was conscious and planned. I don't think having Joey would have been particularly joyous for us if he had come at a time when we were neither financially nor emotionally prepared."

The one-child family is likely to be carefully planned and purposive. In contrast to larger families in which babies often come along at unscheduled and inconvenient intervals, a single child in a family is usually the result of specific intention and careful timing by parents. Because parents tend to plan carefully for their first and only child, the event seems to be happier than the arrival of later children. In one study, 84 per cent of 66 women in their first pregnancies described themselves as "happy," while only 36 per cent of 146 mothers who already had children welcomed a subsequent child.[2]

Being "wanted" is very important for the development of a child. Referring to the formation of a child's character, Drs. A.H. Maslow and Béla Mittelmann have written:

> . . .an important factor is whether the parents want the child. If they do not, if the coming child is unwelcome, there is greater likelihood

of the child's being rejected, at least partially; and this rejection, whether open or hidden, conscious or unconscious, will eventually communicate itself to the child and create in him a feeling of rejection.[3]

Having a planned and wanted child is also important to the happiness and satisfaction of parents. The financial and emotional complications imposed by a second, unplanned child can create unnecessary family tension. "We were in college when our children were born," recalled the father of two. "We planned and prepared for the first child, and everything was great. But two years later my wife insisted we have another child. We weren't ready for a second child, and our souring marriage reflects it."

Studies show that the adjustment of a mother to parenting is particularly influenced by her desire to have the child. Dr. Alice Rossi has found ". . .evidence to date, involving samples of both upper-middle-class private and working-class clinic patients, indicates that difficulty of adjustment is greater with multipara [second or subsequent] than primipara [first] births."[4] In Dr. Rossi's opinion, the adjustment problems with later births occur because the children are "less apt to be wanted by the mothers."[5] Constance, the mother of two daughters and a son, remarked, "Having our first child was my choice. The second I had because my in-laws thought we shouldn't have an only child. The third I had because my husband wanted a son. We should have stopped while we were ahead."

Parents who decide to stop with one child avoid the trauma that can result from subsequent births that are less timely and less welcome. A conscious decision to remain a one-child family gives parents the confidence to withstand pressures to have a second child and declare, as did one mother, "when they invent them potty trained with teeth in their mouths, we'll have another."

Close Relationships

The one-child family is a small world. The limited number of members makes their relationship close and intense. "In a three-person family, you've got to depend on each other," remarked an adult single child. "You don't have many options."

A formula devised by Dr. Jules Henry and Samuel Warson illustrates how the possible number of interactional patterns within a family dramatically increases as more members are added. Their formula is stated as $2_n - n - 1$, with "n" being the total number of members in the family. Using this formula, they show that in the one-child family, four interrelationships are possible—mother-father, mother-child, father-child, and father-mother and child. In a family of four, 11 interrelationships are possible; in a family of five, 26; and in a family of six, 57.[6] Clearly, the one-child family involves fewer relationships and more intensity than larger families.

What are the consequences of this intensity? The most obvious is that the parent-child relationship takes on an overwhelming significance. For the child, parents are his or her only continuing source of reward, feedback, and role models. For parents, the situation is equally intense. Unlike the parent who has several children to satisfy parental expectations, the one-child parent has only one source of parenting satisfaction.

The intensity of the one-child family seems to make crisis events have greater impact on its members because there is no "spreading" effect. For instance, a single child of divorcing parents has no siblings with whom to share the experience. He or she must cope with the divorce alone. "When my folks split, it was the most traumatic experience of my life," remarked a single child. "I didn't talk to anyone about it and blamed it all on myself." By contrast, a woman who was one of three daughters said of her parents' divorce, "My sisters and I decided that my parents were better off divorced, so we made a pact among ourselves to stick together and make it as easy for everyone as we could."

Although intensity can cause some family problems, it also promotes a special closeness between parents and child. Children who grow up in larger families often miss such parent/child closeness. In a 1970 study of adolescents, Ivan Nye, John Carlson, and Gerald Garrett found that children from one-child families had the most positive feelings about their parents and that positive feelings decreased as family size increased.[7] A carpenter with five siblings recalled, "I was often excited about the prospect about doing something special with my father, but somehow he never quite found the time or we had to take along other kids. Consequently I never felt very close to my Dad."

Closeness and intensity are hallmarks of a one-child family. The consequences of this intensive nature can be both positive and negative, but parents choosing to have a single child can anticipate strong family ties. As one single child remarked, "Its hard to get lost in the shuffle when it's a small deck."

Democratic Decision-Making

In addition to being planned and close, the one-child family tends to be democratic. "My parents always took my wishes into consideration," reflected a single child, now an adult. "From vacation spots to curfew, they asked me what I thought—and they listened." The single child develops a sense of being able to influence his or her parents rather than being ruled or dictated by them.

Such democracy is rarely practiced in larger families. To

keep the family functioning efficiently and relatively peacefully, parents having several children are more likely to set rules and insist on obedience.[8] The experience of living in a parent-controlled, role-oriented environment influences children more readily to accept and approve of authoritarianism. When Carmi Schooler rated more than 3,000 American males on characteristics of authoritarianism, she found that the men from large families were more likely to display this trait than men from smaller families.[9] In the Bernice Moore and Wayne Holtzman study of high school students, they found that adolescents who came from larger families more often approved of authoritarian child-rearing practices.[10] A woman who grew up with four siblings told us, "Mom decided and told us what to do. She knew better than to ask the five of us what we would like for dinner or what time we would like to go to bed. It would have been bedlam."

A well-functioning democratic family pattern can be a rewarding experience for parents as well as children. Relieved of pressures to make decisions that are equitable to several children, parents of a single child can relax in their parenting role and allow some of the family decision-making to be carried out by the child. "We often eat dinner out," explained the mother of a four-year-old, "and about once a week we allow our son to decide where we will go. At first he only wanted to go to McDonalds, but now he's learning to take a lot of things into consideration and choose a place he thinks will please all of us. I doubt if we'd let him make this kind of decision if there were other kids in the family."

A one-child family can have an authoritarian parent/child relationship, but it probably will not. Parents choosing to have one child can expect that they will have a more equalitarian relationship with their child than will parents with several children. Dominance is just not as important when only one child is involved. In the words of one mother, "The 'me mother, you kid' syndrome just doesn't seem to fit in the single-child family."

Affluence

Money stretches only so far. The one-child family stretches each dollar a little less than the family with more children. As a result, the one-child family has more money to spend on each member and lives a more affluent life-style than multichild families in the same socioeconomic class. "We always drove to the beach for family vacations," remarked a high school math teacher who was one of three children. "I had a grammar school friend who was an only child. Although his dad had basically the same job as mine, his family flew somewhere for their vacations."

The affluence of one-child families is often further enhanced by the mother's employment outside the home. Less encumbered by child-rearing responsibilities, the mother may well pursue a higher paying career rather than a supplementary job. Interruption of her career, and its income, is less likely with one child than with more.

The availability of more money affects all family members. For the child and each parent, affluence means more individual possessions and opportunities. For the family unit, it means more shared experiences. "We weren't rich," recalled a middle-aged adult only, "but we always had enough money to travel, to go to events in the city, and to buy things that we could all enjoy. I think it was being able to afford to do stimulating things together that made us such a close family." The family affluence may even affect the family's health. When Joe Wray examined how various size families apportioned their income, he found that as family size increases the total medical expenditure per family decreases. Wray concluded that "larger families may be depriving themselves of medical care in order to meet other needs."[11]

To describe the affluence of the one-child family is not to suggest that money is the *raison d'etre* of life. But relative affluence is one predictable consequence of a decision to have a one-child family. The words, "We can't afford it," will be spoken less often in the single-child family than in the multichild family.

Individual Independence

"Although we're a close family, I would say individually we are very independent. While we may be naturally self-reliant, I think our one-child situation encourages our independence." This statement by the mother of one teen-ager points up another feature of the one-child family—more freedom for each family member to pursue independent interests.

This independence is expressed differently by each family member. Being less restricted by nurturing responsibilities, parents can see themselves first as people and second as parents. "I consider mothering just one part—but a very important part—of my life," stated the mother of a single child. "I'm hardly anything but a mother," replied the mother of five children.

The effect of this independence may not be particularly profound for fathers, who have traditionally sought their identity through their careers and have had only a marginal commitment to fatherhood. However, the one-child family increases a father's independence by placing fewer financial and time demands on him.

A mother is more significantly affected by the increased independence allowed in the one-child life-style. Restricted family size enables mothers of one to look outside their family for identity and satisfaction. Dr. Alice Rossi observed that the average woman spends only 39 per cent of her life in the role of mother;[12] that time is further reduced for the mother of a single child. Since the mother in the planned one-child family knows that there will not be an endless stream of children to hug her legs and say, "Mommy," she is more likely to establish an identity independent of her child.

For many mothers that independent identity is expressed in a career outside the home. Having a career identity and commitment helps these women circumvent the "what do I do now?" problem many women face in their early forties when their children leave home and their husbands are absorbed in their work. A psychologist at a mental health clinic observed, "I worked hard while my son was growing up to prepare myself for this job. I went to graduate school for five years, read myself half blind, and wrote a 250-page dissertation. When my son leaves home, I know what I'll be doing." Genevieve Landau, editor-in-chief of *Parents' Magazine*, has commented on the trend toward women seeking an identity independent of their children:

> Now it is no longer necessary for women to demonstrate their femininity and motherliness—their total worth—by numbers [of children], as it were. . . Only part of them, though often the best part, is expressed in caring for their children. Part is also expressed in the things they like to do, be it golf, gardening, or geophysics, work in the kitchen, or work in the lab. Women know that to be good mothers they must have a good feeling about themselves as people.[13]

The third person to be considered in family independence is, of course, the child. If mother and father are both "doing their thing," what happens to the child?

In general, single children seem to develop the same independent characteristics exhibited by their parents. When Michael Masterson used a personality test to determine how much 155 college students sought approval from others for their actions, he found that student "need for approval" increased as family size increased.[14] In other words, the smaller the family the more independent the child.

By having opportunity to make decisions, the single child develops confidence in independent actions. Stimulated by observing the personal pursuits of his or her parents, the child is encouraged to develop his or her own interests and resources. The result generally is an independent, self-confident individual who feels sure of his or her parents' love and is confident in setting the course of his or her own life.

Personal Consequences: A Summary

In preceding chapters as well as in this one, many aspects of the one-child family have been discussed. To help synthesize this information, we have identified 12 personal consequences, positive and negative, that you and your partner can *expect* if you decide to have one child.

Expected Positive Consequences:

1. Your child's intellectual, emotional, and social development will be equal to, and in some instances superior to, that of children coming from larger families.
2. Your marriage will be as happy as the marriages of couples with more children—and maybe happier.
3. Your family life-style will be more affluent than that of other families in the same income class.
4. Your parent/child relationship will be close and intense.
5. Your family life-style will be planned and democratic.
6. You, your spouse, and your child will be quite independent.

Expected Negative Consequences:

1. Your child will miss the unique experience of sibling relationships.
2. Your child will grow up in an adult world of high expectations.
3. Your child will place demands on you for companionship.
4. As parents, you will have only one opportunity to "make good" at parenting.
5. Rearing one child will be unsatisfying if you (particularly a mother) do not pursue independent interests.
6. Since the rewards of parenthood are often delayed, you may wish in later life you had had more children—and wishing will be all you can do.

We have listed the consequences as positive and negative, but in reality none is exclusively good or bad. Instead, each has the potential to be both. Whether the consequences are viewed as positive or negative depends on the needs, expectations, and perceptions of the couple considering them. "Everything about the one-child family (or any family for that matter), depends on what you make of it," theorized the mother of one youngster. "If you believe the one-child family is a good way of life, you will make it so. If you believe it is harmful, you will probably make it turn out that way."

The One-Child Family: Two Life-style Examples

Positive and negative consequences of the one-child family occur in different patterns for different families. An inside look at two family styles—the traditional and the equalitarian—helps to illustrate some of those differences.

The Traditional Family

Ron and Linda Boyd have been married four years and live in a new subdivision on the West Coast. An accountant, Ron has an office in University Park and earns approximately $15,000 per year. Linda is a full-time housewife and mother of their two-year-old son, Mike.

Home to Ron is "the place I'd rather be than anywhere else." After arriving home from work about 5:30, he sips a beer and reads the evening paper when Mike is not climbing on his lap. Linda shares Ron's feelings about their home life. Aside from church, most of their time is spent edging the sidewalk, mulching the flowers, and watering the grass. Their latest project is to build a sandbox for Mike and fence in the backyard with some wire they got at a truckload sale.

Their roles are fairly rigid. Ron is responsible for their income; Linda does all the banking and pays the bills. Ron takes care of the car and garbage; Linda does the shopping, prepares the meals, does the laundry, and cleans the house.

"Since Ron needs his sleep, I have always taken care of Mike. I don't think Ron knows how to change a diaper," remarks Linda.

Because Linda and Ron are both active church members, their friends are neither "his" nor "hers." Last Saturday their Sunday school class met at one member's farm for a day of picnicking and skipping rocks on the lake. Mike enjoyed feeding small fish at the water's edge.

Although the Boyds are generally happy with their lives, they do acknowledge certain problems. The major one is economic. Ron makes a good salary, but their mortgage and car payments gobble it up. He sometimes questions Linda about their constantly depleted checking account. "If you want to know what happens to all the money, you keep up with it," Linda snaps back. "You're the accountant."

The Boyd's other major problem is philosophical. Ron and Linda live in different worlds. He leaves for the office at 7:15 and spends the rest of the day accounting for every nickel his company spends. When he returns from a harrowing day with the auditor, he doesn't understand why Linda is in such a bad mood. "She's just been home all day drinking coffee and playing with Mike," he muses.

The implication that she loafs through the day irritates Linda. She believes that her tasks of keeping house and caring for a young child are tiring and frustrating responsibilities. "Mike is going through the 'no' stage, and it's difficult to cope with," remarks Linda. "By the time Ron gets home, I feel like I have given a quart of blood."

Because Ron's day is spent at the office and Linda's day is spent at home, each feels "I'm doing all the work." Their limited perspectives prevent them from understanding each other's concerns. Their traditional relationship will not allow them to consider a meshing of roles, such as his helping with the housework in exchange for her seeking part-time employment.

Although Mike is now oblivious to his parents' roles, in years to come he will learn that women, wives, and mothers

are people who stay home, take care of babies, and prepare
fried chicken for the church picnic. Men, husbands, and
fathers are people who earn money away from home, participate little in household responsibilities, and gripe about
what the wife hasn't been doing all day.

In the traditional marriage, as in any marriage, the partners may have one of four reactions to their first baby. Both
may express delight in their new son or daughter, only the
mother may be enamored, only the father may be pleased, or
both may be dismayed at the child's entrance into the family
unit. In the Boyd's case, Linda loves her new son, but Ron is
rather ambivalent. "Although I really get a rush when Mike
hugs me and says, 'Daddy,' he has affected my relationship
with Linda," Ron explains. "She's tired all the time, and we
don't spend as much time together as we used to—you can't
with a baby in the house."

The Boyd household exemplifies some—but not all—of
the common characteristics of one-child families. Mike was a
planned baby. Since his arrival, the three family members
have become very close. The meaning of life for Ron and
Linda revolves around each other and their son. Aside from
camping during the summer, evenings and weekends are
spent at home; cocktail parties, restaurants, and movies do
not interest the Boyds. Their needs are met inside the family.

Unlike other members of one-child families, Linda and
Ron have few independent interests. She attends an exercise
class three days per week and Ron is a member of the local
Toastmaster's Club, but most of their activities and conversations center on Mike, TV, and church. Although the Boyds
are as affluent as other families in Ron's salary range, inflation has gnawed away at their discretionary income, leaving
them little money to pursue personal interests.

Why are the Boyds a one-child family? Since the traditional family is by definition child-centered, having only one
child may be unusual. Linda explains their decision this way.

"Several considerations went into our resolution to stop
with one. Money was a big part of it. But even more impor-

tant was our attitude about parenting. While we love Mike dearly, we also love each other, and in many ways Mike places restrictions on our marital relationship. We just can't give each other as much time or attention as we used to. If we had another child, our relationship would be further interrupted. It seems like a selfish decision, but we feel it's the right one."

The Equalitarian Family

Just as all aspirins are not alike, neither are all one-child families. The life-style of the Washington family is quite different from that of the Boyds. Jenny and John Washington and their eight-year-old daughter, Connie, live in a western Chicago suburb. John is an attorney for a large grocery chain, and Jenny is the director of a federally funded, visiting nurse program. Connie attends a public elementary school near the family's three-bedroom condominium.

Jenny and John have worked hard to get where they are today. Childhood sweethearts, the Washingtons married soon after graduating from high school. Rather than settling for assembly-line jobs, the couple vowed that each of them would get a college education. "For the next ten years," recalls Jenny, "we struggled to keep in school by working at part-time jobs and getting minority student loans."

After Jenny finished her nurse's training, she went to work while John continued on to law school. In her first year of nursing, Jenny became pregnant. "It was a big surprise," she remembers. "I had some medical problems which supposedly made it impossible for me to conceive."

The Washingtons met the news of a baby's pending arrival with mixed feelings. "We were both excited about having a child, but the timing was bad and we were concerned about how we could continue our career plans and care for a child also," remarks John.

The first two years of Connie's life were a difficult adjust-

ment. Jenny continued to work and was soon promoted to a
supervisory position, which required her to spend much
more time at her job. To save on child care expenses, John
arranged his law school schedule so that he could stay with
Connie while Jenny worked. "We both adored Connie,"
Jenny says, "but during those first two years neither of us
had undivided time to give her."

The Washingtons believe that their early experience with
parenting has greatly influenced the life-style they have
today. "If I had stayed home when Connie was born," remarks Jenny, "I think things might be different now. As it
was, I had to work, and the more I worked, the more I liked
it. When John finished law school, I could have quit, but I
didn't want to. By then I was well entrenched in my career."

It was at this point that the Washingtons considered, and
decided against, having a second child. "Connie was getting
old enough to go places with us and was becoming quite
self-sufficient. We just didn't want to start through the
diaper and bottle stage again," said John.

What is the Washington's life-style like today? "I guess you
would call ours an equalitarian family," John states. "Since
we've never experienced the situation in which I worked and
Jenny stayed home, we've arrived at a pretty equal sharing of
tasks and responsibilities."

In practice, the Washingtons' arrangement requires a
fairly structured daily schedule for all three family members.
Jenny rises at 6:00 a.m. After dressing for work, she straight-
ens up the house or does a load of laundry. However, most of
the housework is done by a housekeeper who comes weekly.

John's morning routine calls for him to take care of breakfast for himself and Connie (Jenny doesn't eat breakfast).
Some mornings he prepares breakfast at home; other mornings he and Connie eat at a neighborhood cafe.

The Washington household is empty by 8:00 a.m., and the
three family members are seldom in contact during the day.
When school is out at 3:00 p.m., Connie goes home with a

schoolmate and waits until one of her parents comes for her. "We still pay for after-school care because we .feel better about it, and Connie's happier being with a friend," explains Jenny.

Evenings are very irregular for the Washingtons. Jenny's work keeps her at the office one or two evenings a week. John also often works late. In addition, Jenny attends a weekly art class, and John has a standing handball game. The spouses try to work out their individual schedules so that one of them is home with Connie, but that isn't always possible. On evenings when both parents are away, Connie stays overnight with her friend.

"I guess by traditional standards," Jenny reflects, "our life-style is not very home-oriented. Meals around the family table are not important to us. When we have time for recreation, we prefer things away from home."

"Financially we don't lead a very frugal life-style," says John. "We spend a lot on eating out and entertainment, but that's how we like to live." The Washington's life-style is possible because the combined incomes of John and Jenny are more than $45,000 per year.

How does Connie fit into the lives of Jenny and John? "To answer that honestly," replies Jenny, "I'd have to say that Connie is an important part of our individual lives and our marital relationship, but she is not the central focus in either instance. We both have many other interests, and our careers are particularly important to us. As a result neither of us can be solely dedicated to Connie's nurture."

John adds, "Our relationship with Connie and our family unit changes as she grows older. When she was young, it seemed like our entire life revolved around getting babysitters. Jenny and I used to get into enormous power plays about who would take care of Connie. Now that she's older, many of our former conflicts just don't occur."

How do the Washingtons feel about the one-child family? Jenny's response is quick. "I can't imagine any other way of

life for us. I love my child immensely, but I simply do not
have the time, energy, or interest that another child would
require."

"I agree," John replies. "I think our situation boils down to
the fact that we've both got a lot of things going in life. We
can raise one child—raise her well I believe—but we don't
think we can deal with more children. While Connie may not
get some of the things in our life-style that she would in a
more traditional family, we're pleased with the kind of person she's becoming."

Society and the One-Child Family

Having considered the personal outcomes you can expect if
you decide to have one child, we turn to the effects of the
one-child family on society. What consequences can society
expect if more couples choose to limit their families to one
child?

Reduction of the Population Crisis

Paul Ehrlich observed, "The explosive growth of the human
population is the most significant terrestrial event of the past
million millenia. Three and one-half billion people now inhabit the earth, and every year this number increases by 70
million."[15] In America we have about 210 million people and
are expected to have close to 270 million by the year 2000.[16]
These numbers foretell crowded cities, more pollution, and
an incessant drain on natural resources.

Population experts advocate a two-child family norm as a
means of stabilizing population growth, but an increase in
the number of one-child families would further reduce the
crisis level. A 1972 report by the Presidential Commission on
Population Growth and the American Future projected that
an immediate adoption of a one-child family norm would

cause the American population to crest at about 220 million in 1990; then the population would fall rapidly. Although such a shift would, according to the Commission, bring some important immediate benefits, such as more classroom space and less economic pressure on family heads, it would eventually result in many labor and production surpluses. These and other changes might well necessitate restructuring segments of our economy.[17]

Some people fear that increased popularity of the one-child family would create another type of crisis—a society overrun with lower class, poor, uneducated people. This concern is based on a belief that middle-class couples would be most likely to limit their child-bearing, while lower class couples would continue to reproduce in greater numbers.

Recent analysis of population trends indicate that restricted reproduction will not lead to an imbalance of social classes. Analyzing the Current Population Surveys of 1967–1971, Dr. Frederick Jaffe, Director of the Center for Family Planning Program Development, found that the birth rates for poverty-level mothers, although still higher than for high-income mothers, were declining at a faster rate.[18] Looking specifically at minority groups, Dr. James Sweet, Director for the Center for Demography and Ecology at the University of Wisconsin, Madison, concluded: "The continuous decline in fertility in the United States since 1957, while affecting all elements of the population, has been most pronounced and most rapid among those groups which previously had the highest fertility—blacks, American Indians, and Mexican Americans—all of whom experienced fertility declines more rapid than those experienced by urban whites between 1957–1960 and 1967–1970."[19] Both Jaffe and Sweet attributed the declining rates to the introduction of more efficient contraceptives, social approval of their use, and the establishment of federal programs to give poor people easier access to birth control information and contraceptives.

Although not advocating that the one-child family be adopted as the standard American family size, we do believe that our society would benefit from the population reduction that would occur if more parents chose to have one child.

The critical nature of the population problem makes it imperative that all citizens be personally concerned about the number of people who inhabit our environment. As Ehrlich has said, "Whatever your cause, it's a lost cause without population control."[20]

Fewer Unwanted Children

In addition to population control, an increase in the number of one-child families would result in fewer unwanted children. Information gathered in the 1970 National Fertility Study conducted by the Office of Population Research at Princeton University revealed that *15* per cent of *all* births from 1966 to 1970 were described as "unwanted" by the parents. However, only *1* per cent of *first* births were described as unwanted.[21]

Although the term "unwanted child" conjures up the image of a teen-age mother with an out-of-wedlock baby, many unwanted children are born into stable family units. The accidental or "impulse" conception happens just as easily to married as unmarried couples. Even when parents describe their child as "wanted," the couple's motivations for having that child do not always suggest a child wanted for its own sake. For example, does having a baby to please grandparents, to save a marriage, or to try for a child of the opposite sex make a child truly "wanted"? And what about the second child that is conceived to "save the first." Is such a child wanted for itself or to relieve parents' anxiety about having an "only child"?

If the social stigma of the one-child family were removed and parents felt comfortable about a decision to have a single child, it is less likely that some second, less-wanted children would be born. (One unwanted child is too many.) In a time when overpopulation threatens the quality of life for everyone, the world can afford only children who are "wanted" for the very best of reasons.

Friendships Substituted for "Siblingships"

In describing different kinds of relationships among people, sociologists speak of interactions among family members as "primary" relationships; relationships with persons outside the family unit are referred to as "secondary." Because the number of primary relationships is limited in a one-child family, single children tend to develop and value secondary relationships more than do children from multichild families. In a society having more single children, friendships may take on the importance of sibling relationships.

What might this mean for social networks in our society? It could mean that friendship networks would grow stronger, that families would think less in terms of biological relations and more in terms of shared interests. Living arrangements (apartment complexes, planned single-home areas, communal housing) in which children could easily share companionship might be sought more often. Children's friendships would be taken more seriously. Parents would consider their child's friends not just as playmates, but as important socializers, sources of necessary feedback and support. By including other children more often and more closely in their family activities, parent's concerns and rewards might be extended from their own child to other children within their friendship network. In other words, family circles could grow beyond blood ties.

An example of what could happen for an individual one-child family was illustrated when Dean, now an adult single child, described his childhood experience:

> I grew up next door to another only child, Harold, who was one year younger than I. Our parents had been friends before we were born, and Harold and I fit right into their friendship. Either of us

was always welcome at the other's house. In fact, we never even knocked when we went back and forth. We spent holidays together and often the two families vacationed together. Our parents felt free to correct or discipline both of us, and they often did. Harold even got my hand-me-downs.

Because of our close relationship, we developed many of the same characteristics of brothers. We were brutally frank with each other, but we would also rush to the other's defense in an instant. We knew each other's parents well enough to be able to commiserate about our parent problems and to share our innermost thoughts.

Although we live many miles apart now, we're still best friends. We talk on the phone at least once a week and see each other a couple of times a year. Since our parents are all dead now, Harold and his family often spend Christmas with me and my family.

People tell me there's no substitute for a "blood brother," but as far as I'm concerned Harold and I have as good a relationship as any brothers ever had.

Adult-Oriented Society

Figures from the Bureau of Census show that 45 per cent of our population is now under 25 years of age and that 10 per cent is over 65. Demographers project that by the year 2000, as our population growth approaches zero, only one-third of all Americans will be under age 25,[22] and persons over 65 will comprise 20 per cent of the population.[23]

These figures are based on a two-child family norm. The adoption of a one-child family norm would produce an even more dramatic result. The report by the Presidential commission on Population Growth suggests that if the one-child family did soon become the most prevalent family size in our society, by the year 2050, 60-year-olds would outnumber one-year-olds three to one.[24]

One can only speculate about the changes that would result from a turnaround in the ratio of young to old people. As one possibility, our society would become less youth-oriented and perhaps even less youth-worshiping. Family life would tend to revolve around the interests of the parents rather than those of the child, and children might be drawn earlier into the adult world.

Our society has never had a one-child family norm, and the consequences of a significant increase in the number of one-child families are not completely predictable. However, it appears that both the demography and the nature of our society would be altered if more couples chose to have one child. Although some changes might be difficult, the advantages seem to outweigh the disadvantages.

A Society of One-Child Families?

It is unlikely that the one-child family will become the standard American family size, at least in the near future. The 1977 Gallup poll findings cited earlier show that only two per cent of the respondents felt that the one-child family was ideal.[25] After reviewing this data, Dr. Judith Blake wrote in the journal *Demography*:

> . . .there is an overwhelming consensus among white Americans concerning the disadvantage experienced by an only child. Such a degree of consensus leads us to speculate that informal social controls may operate openly and strongly against those couples who intend (or are even considering) having one child. Grandparents, friends, pediatricians, ministers, teachers, babysitters—the entire roster of socially significant individuals who are in intimate contact with young parents—can feel secure in openly expressing the belief that it is "unfair" to have an only child if one can avoid it. This is a belief that just about everyone shares.[26]

Although America's present reproducing population shows little inclination to embrace the one-child family concept, younger Americans may be more favorably disposed. Two studies conducted by the Gilbert Youth Research Organization focused on a national probability sample of young Americans between the ages of 14 and 25. In 1972, six per cent of both males and females expressed a preference for the one-child family. In 1974, the percentage had increased to 10.[27] These young people seem to be reevaluating the single child phenomenon and finding it more attractive.

American attitudes toward the one-child family are not universal. In the U.S.S.R., the single-child family is now the most common family size. Small apartments, career wives, and tight budgets have convinced most Russians to make their first child also their last.[28]

In the United States, the two-child family norm will continue, at least for the foreseeable future. However, perhaps as pressures to restrict population increase and more positive information about single children becomes known, American parents will take a fresh look at the advantages of the one-child life-style. The single-child family will not soon replace the two-child family as the most popular family size, but it may soon begin to make a better showing.

Making the One-Child Decision

While emphasizing that the one-child family is a desirable life-style for today's world, we do not believe that the one-child family is "right" for everyone. Some couples will choose to be childfree, while others will want "a house full of children." Our concern is that couples feel "free" to have a single child if that is what they want.

In some marriages, spouses may disagree about the desirability of the one-child family. When this situation occurs, the problem must be resolved like the mating of two porcupines—with difficulty and great care. Ranking values (marriage and desired number of children) is essential. The ultimate question is, "Do I want to have a single child and am I willing to dissolve our relationship if my partner does not agree with me?"

Unless one of the spouses is involved in an extramarital relationship with someone who shares his or her value about family size and offers the promise of remarriage, it is unlikely that the marriage will break over the additional child issue. Because of the magnitude of this decision, a qualified marriage counselor should be consulted to help the partners evaluate their personal and marital values in relation to a second child.[29]

The one-child family style seems most suitable for those couples who want to experience parenthood, while also retaining ample opportunity to pursue personal interests or careers. It is also appropriate for couples who value close parent/child relationships and for parents to whom a self-confident, independent child and a more affluent life-style are more important than a second chance to "make good" at parenting.

The crucial issue in a decision about family size "is not how many children are right for a given family, but rather what kind of human beings that family can turn out."[30] Any couple who believes that having a single child offers them the best potential for producing a happy, healthy child and a satisfying parenting experience should make the one-child decision—and they should feel confident in their decision.

two / *Rearing*
the Single Child

six / *The Single Child from Infancy through Adolescence*

The problems which an only child faces are essentially those faced by all human beings.[1]

NORMA E. CUTTS AND NICHOLAS MOSELEY

One day in a pediatrician's office two women began to talk about their children.

"I've got five kids," said one of the women. "I love them all dearly, but sometimes I think if I have to buy another pair of shoes, pick up another toy, or sit through another doctor's appointment, I'll go off the deep end."

Then she asked her new confidante how many children she had.

"One son," was the reply.

"Oh, my dear," said the mother of five. "It must be terribly difficult to have an only child. How do you raise him?"

"The same way you raise your five," answered the other woman, "but I only do it a fifth as much."

Rearing a single child is basically the same as rearing any other child—diapers must be changed, skinned knees bandaged, and anxiety about teen-age romances relieved. However, there are some special rearing considerations which result from the absence of other children in the household.

In this chapter we will draw on the experiences and views of single-child parents to discuss the particular needs of single children at various stages of their development.

The First Two Years

For the first two years, a single child is like any other baby. Feeding, diapering, bathing, and cuddling make up the child's day. An array of illnesses ranging from colic to measles interrupt the usual routines. Providing stimulating experiences while protecting the household from total disarray keeps parents constantly on the move.

Like the parents of any first child, single-child parents are generally inexperienced in the day-to-day care of their child. This inexperience can make daily baby routines seem unrelenting, and any problem may take on crisis proportions. But these frustrations are counterbalanced by the novelty of having a new baby, and for most parents this experience turns parenting into a challenging adventure.

Special Rearing Considerations

Although many parents do not make the one-child decision during the first two years of their child's life, the kind of relationship they develop with their child during these years will greatly influence their parent/child experiences if they later decide to stop with one.

Parenting patterns. "I was a child development major in college, so I had lots of ideas about how I would rear my child," explained one mother. "What the books didn't tell me was that I would be so overwhelmed with the demands of my child that I'd never have time to reflect on whether I was taking a 'laissez-faire' or 'authoritarian' approach. Yet I realize that I unconsciously established certain patterns very early with my child. Unfortunately not all of them were good."

One of the joys, and dangers, of parenting is that parents can make up their own rules. Although there is no "right" way to parent a single child (or any child), the early parenting patterns set the tone for later relationships. The one-child parents we interviewed emphasized the importance of establishing two patterns with a single child from the very beginning. One is to develop a sense of proportion about the child and your responsibilities as a parent. "You've got to sort out what's important and what's not important from the start," said one father. "That's pretty hard to do when you haven't had any experience, but it's necessary. If you don't you'll keep yourselves and your child living in constant crisis."

A sense of proportion relates to everything from how important it is to bathe the baby each day to whether the child's temperature warrants a 3:00 a.m. phone call to the doctor. When asked how parents can develop a realistic perspective, one older mother replied, "Well, I would sit back and ask myself, 'Now if I had five kids would I be making a big deal out of this?' "

The other pattern discussed by parents is allowing the child an appropriate amount of independence. "With an only child, or any first child, parents have a hard time easing up on the reins," reflected the mother of an adult only. "I think you have to start letting go the minute they're born."

"Letting go" of the very young child includes allowing that child to take some risks—to get down from the kitchen table alone, to wander into the grass even though there may be stickers, to take a tumble with an older child in a playful wrestling match, to spend the night with a relative or sitter. These events begin to establish a pattern that allows the child to see him- or herself as an individual apart from parents and helps parents to realize that their function is to guide, not envelop.

Individual relationships with the child. "I'm not very good with babies," one father was heard telling a friend, "so I've decided to let my wife pretty much raise the kid until he's old enough so I can take him fishing. Then I'll take over."

If the father follows through with his plan, he may find that his five-year-old son has little interest in him when he's ready to "take over." Parents who wish to have good relationships with their children should begin developing those relationships early. Because the single child has a limited number of family associations, it is vital that the child have a strong individual relationship with each parent.

In traditional families, a close bond between mother and child seems to develop easily since the mother spends many hours caring for the child. For a father or working mother, the bond is not automatically established, and it requires conscious planning.

"When Elly was just a couple of months old, my wife and I agreed that I would take care—complete care—of her every Saturday from the time she got up until bedtime," explained one father. "Truthfully, I hated it at first. It was a lot of work and I resented giving up my time. Now Elly's eight. We still spend every Saturday together, and I really look forward to it as a highlight of my week."

Marriage patterns. One profound, and often unexpected, effect of having a child is the impact of the baby on the parents' marriage. Gone are the days of spontaneous nights on the town, leisurely candlelight dinners, and sleep-late Saturday mornings. How parents cope with this change is crucial to their future family and marital happiness.

"When our daughter was born," said Lorraine, "I would not let her out of my sight. I refused to hire a sitter or even to leave her with my mother. The result? We stayed home for two years.

"Finally," continued Lorraine, "my husband said, 'Amy is driving a wedge between us. Either we start having some kind of life together, or I'm leaving.' I gave in, but our marriage is still suffering the aftereffects of the two-year black-out."

Maintaining a good marriage relationship is important no matter how many children are involved, but it is especially critical that one-child parents not allow their child to make their marriage a "threesome." If parents don't immediately establish their need for, and right to, an adult relationship independent of the child, the single child will come to believe that he or she must be included in all the parents' activities, and parents will feel guilty when they don't include the child. The result is predictable—a deterioration of the parents' relationship and the emergence of a skillful manipulator.

A Healthy Beginning

Although parents may not decide to have a single child until their first child is older, if they develop a sense of proportion about child-rearing, establish individual relationships with the child, and keep their marriage thriving during the first two years of the child's life, they will have a healthy foundation for parenting a single child. As the child matures, these early patterns will help them to deal with the later problems of rearing a single child.

The Preschool Years (Ages 3-5)

About the age of three, children begin to "turn into human beings." They walk, speak their needs and concerns, use the toilet, accomplish simple tasks for themselves, and begin to develop some sense of themselves and their place in the family.

It is during their firstborn's preschool years that many parents make a family size decision. In deciding whether to have a second child, parents often become avid observers of their firstborn. Meticulously comparing their child with other children, parents look for signs of maladjustment that might result from the child's lack of siblings.

In their observations, most parents find that their child is much like other children. Having passed through the "terrible twos," the three-year-old child seems to take a positive attitude toward life, seeks to please parents rather than defy them, and begins to enjoy playing with, rather than just being around, other children. At four, the child is likely to enter another trying period in which verbal fits are not uncommon, a need to kick, hit, or break everything in sight obsesses him or her, and the child's imagination runs wild. This period is followed by a more calm and reasonable year when the child turns five.

One difference parents may notice is that their single child seems more adultlike than children the same age who have siblings. Seventy per cent of the parents in our survey believed that their single children acted more mature than other children (Appendix 2). Almost always, single children have a greater language facility, relate more easily to adults, and act more "grown up" when in an adult situation.

"By the time our son was four," recalled the mother of a teen-age son, "he was able to order in a restaurant and take the check with the money to the cashier by himself. I didn't see many other four-year-olds doing that."

As the preschooler begins to play regularly with other children, parents also may notice that the child is less competitive than his or her friends who have siblings. Having never had to compete for personal possessions or parents' attention, the single child may watch with amazement as his or her friends bicker and vie for possessions. The child may jump into the fray to find out what it is all about, or he or she may retreat from the situation.

Finally, parents may observe that their preschooler has more imaginary friends than other children. Although studies show that as many as 30 per cent of all children have imaginary companions at some time,[2] single children seem more prone to have such imaginations, perhaps because they spend long periods of time by themselves or because their imaginations are stimulated by more books and experiences. Unless the child is excluding other children in favor of these imaginary companions, there is no reason to regard the imaginary playmates as unhealthy.

Special Rearing Considerations

Although the preschooler begins to move outside the home more, parents remain the most important influence in his or her life. At this stage of development, it is important that the parent/child relationship be *assuring* without being *overprotective*, and *encouraging* without being *overexpecting*

Assuring vs. overprotecting. One of the most dangerous tendencies of parents is to overprotect their preschool single child. Lucille's story is a case in point.

> Because my mother was a career woman and didn't spend much time with me, I decided I would give my life to my daughter. I could not do enough for her. Home became her palace and I was her slave. When she started kindergarten, she hated it. She would run away and come home, where I let her watch TV and eat cookies to help her overcome her anxiety about school. Only with the help of an excellent school counselor did I come to realize that I was making my daughter an emotional cripple.

Parents of single children seem to fall rather easily into the overprotection trap. Their child is terribly important to them, and they fear "doing something wrong" in rearing their son or daughter. Without the diversion of another child, their concern can quickly become excessive. To assess whether they are being too protective, parents should look for these signs:

1. Excessive contact between parents and child—child regularly sleeping with parents, holding the child's hand when there is no danger, constantly keeping the child in sight.

2. Prolonging infantile care—feeding the child after he or she is able to do it alone, bathing and dressing the child when he or she is capable, cleaning up after the child, and so on.

3. Interrupting independent behavior—not letting the child complete a task without intervention, not allowing him or her to work out disagreements with other children, and so on.

4. Lack or excess of parental control—giving into the child's every whim by never saying "no," or insisting on complete obedience in avoiding risks and remaining a "baby."[3]

Encouraging vs. overexpecting. The tendency for single children to be observably more adultlike than other children their age often leads to a second pitfall of one-child parenting—expecting too much of the child.

"When Kevin was three, he could carry on an intelligent conversation with any adult," said Alice of her single child. "When he started to school I expected him to handle relations with other children with ease. But he was unable to do so. His teacher said he either stayed completely away from them or provoked them into fights. I just couldn't understand how he could get along with adults so well but could not make it with children."

Although single children may appear more adultlike than other children, their behavior is often pseudo-sophistication parading as true maturity. Because the adultlike behavior is deceiving, parents come to expect mature behavior from the child constantly. If at some point the youngster "acts like a child," adults express disappointment, and the child becomes frustrated.

How can parents make sure their expectations for their child are realistic rather than exaggerated, encouraging rather than overexpecting? Answering the following questions can help.

1. Is your child's behavior (both pleasing and displeasing) in line with the behavior of other children the same age? For example, does your

three-year-old refuse to share his or her possessions because he or she is spoiled, or do all three-year-olds seem excessively selfish?

2. Are your expectations for your child's behavior based on the child's "good" or your convenience? For example, do you expect your 10-year-old to start his or her homework without prodding because it is important for character development or because it would be more pleasant for you if you did not have to remind him or her?

3. Are your expectations for your child significantly higher (or lower) than those of other adults with whom the child has contact? For example, do you continue to insist that your child take advanced math despite his or her teacher's and guidance counselor's assessments that the child should take business math?

Neighborhood play. A single child's first experiences away from home and parents are usually in the neighborhood. As a child becomes trustworthy and confident enough to leave his or her parents' sight for short periods, the neighborhood begins to open new horizons, and he or she discovers others the same age.

Playing with neighborhood children is significant because it marks the first time that the child has an opportunity to make his or her own way. The experience may be painful for the child if he or she is not immediately accepted in the group, and it may be equally as painful for parents to see their child subjected to the "natural," but often unsympathetic, words and actions of other children. But such experiences will (and must) occur.

Parents who have overprotected their children may begin to see the results of that action in their child's reluctance to play with other children. The child may completely refuse to join other children, or he or she may venture into the vicinity of the play area but stay on the fringe of the children's activities. Parents who have experienced a reticent child suggest some helpful strategies: taking the child into the group and introducing him or her to the other children; inviting the children into the child's home so he or she can interact on familiar territory; singling out one child and helping the two children interact on a one-to-one basis.

Parents who have given their child an overdose of self-importance may find that they have a demanding bully who is rejected by other children. Some parents who observed bullying or selfish behavior in their child said that they took direct action by making him or her stop playing. Others said that they talked with their child about the incident or ignored the behavior. Parents who ignored the behavior assumed that their child would "get his (or hers)" from one of the older children.

Whatever the situation, it is important for parents to recognize that their child's relationship with peers reflects his or her relationship with them. If the child has problems with other children, the parents should look carefully at whether they are overindulging or overprotecting their child. They are, after all, his or her ultimate sounding board in life. Their attitudes and responses are most important to the single child. They cannot run interference for their child in all relationships, but they can make certain that the parent/child relationship is healthy and well balanced.

Preschool. When discussing the three- to five-year-old single child, most one-child parents agree on one point—preschool is a good idea. Eighty per cent of the parents in our study had sent their single child to preschool, and all of them felt that it had been a useful experience (Appendix 2).

Most believed that the main benefit of preschool for their child had been the experience of interacting with other children. "If a child has brothers and sisters in the home," said one mother, "there is built-in play with other children. But the single child doesn't automatically have experience with others his own age, so it's important that parents provide this experience in preschool or other organized settings. Without a regular school situation, it's too easy for parents to just let the child stay around the house with them."

In addition to experience with other children, a preschool can give a single child his or her first regular contact with an adult other than parents. "My child and I had developed a real overdependency," confessed the mother of one daughter. "It nearly killed me to see her go to preschool, but sending her was a good decision. She became very fond of her teacher, I had some free time to develop my own interests, and we both began to loosen our hold on each other. I'm not sure that would have happened if we'd waited two more years until Cherry was old enough for first grade.

Sexual development. During the preschool years, children become aware of their bodies and show some interest in reproduction. The single child's questions about sex will not be radically different from other children's, but parents should be aware that their single child has two disadvantages in sex education.

First, since there are no other children in the home, the single child has no constant companion with whom to discuss bodies and sex or to play the "show" game. Therefore, the single child may demonstrate a seemingly excessive interest in parents' or friends' bodies. This interest should not be misinterpreted by parents as an unhealthy preoccupation; it should be understood as the child's way of acquiring a normal amount of information.

Second, the single child will not have the experience of having a new brother or sister in the household. In a multichild family, the mother's pregnancy and the birth of a new sibling provide a natural introduction for a discussion of sex and reproduction. In his book, *Raising the Only Child*, Dr. Murray Kappelman suggests that parents compensate for the single child's lack of a new baby brother or sister by using the occasion of a family friend's pregnancy to initiate a discussion of sex or to follow through on the child's questions.[4]

Preparing a Child to Move into the World

The preschool years are ones of preparing a child physically and psychologically for the experiences he or she will face when leaving the warm nest and entering the new world of school. If parents have prepared their child by loosening their parental grip and providing some preparatory experiences with other children, both parents and child can look forward to the school years as a time of growth and fun.

The Early School Years (Ages 6–12)

Starting school is a major event in the life of any child, but it is especially significant for the single child who has not had preschool experience. Entering school marks the first time that the child must truly cope without parents' intervention.

For single children who emerge from their preschool years with a healthy self-concept and appropriate social skills, school becomes a rewarding, happy experience. Single children tend to achieve well in school, seeking approval from teachers as they have from parents. A recent doctoral dissertation study of elementary teachers' attitudes suggests that single children can expect a generally positive reaction from their teachers. In this study Robert Watford found the teachers' attitudes about single children more positive than those reflected in surveys of the general population.[5]

Through contact with other children in school, the single child begins to develop a heightened sense of family. Other children's reports of new baby brothers or sisters trigger awareness in the single child that he or she is different because he or she has no siblings.

"I'll never forget the day when Stuart was in the first grade, and he came home from school crying his eyes out," recalled one mother. "It seems the kids had been teasing him about being an 'only child,' and not knowing what that meant, he thought he had some deformity. It was the first time he had any sense of not having something other kids had."

As their awareness of not having brothers or sisters increases in their early school years, single children seem to develop an extra need for a sense of family. Family traditions become very important to them. Cousins or other relatives, especially those near in age, are relished. Close family friends also are eagerly courted by the child. All these efforts are the child's way of defining and perhaps expanding his or her family experiences.

As in preschool years, the school-age single child generally seems more adultlike than other children. Parents report that their single children have more adultlike senses of humor, are more interested in participating in adult activities, and function more smoothly in all-adult situations. However, the mannerisms are still "pseudo," and single children can be regularly expected to "act their age"—often to the dismay of parents spoiled by their child's usual adultlike behavior.

Special Rearing Considerations

When the life of the single child becomes three-dimensional with school, peers, and family activities, the child's needs begin to change, and special rearing considerations must be made.

Making school a positive experience. Like all first children, a single child begins school without "preconditioning" by older siblings. Although he or she may hear some stories about school from neighborhood friends, for the most part the single child begins school with only the notions suggested by parents. It is, therefore, crucial that parents lay the groundwork for a positive experience. A first-grade teacher with many years of experience made these suggestions:

> Because the only child has no siblings to explain the ropes, his or her parents should prepare the child by discussing what can be expected at school. But they should be careful to make their description realistic—not so intimidating that the child is overwhelmed or so exciting that the teacher can't live up to the expectation. Parents also should avoid making it seem that the whole classroom will revolve

around the child. School should be described as a place where the child will share learning experiences with others."

Parent-teacher communication. "My son's kindergarten teacher taught me as much as she did him," recalled one mother. "With her understanding of children and her observation of Roy with other kids, she helped me develop a better perspective of him—his strengths and weaknesses. Together we were able to get him off to a good start in school."

Parent-teacher communication is vital in the development of a single child, at every age level. A child's teacher can see him or her in relation to other children and can help parents develop more realistic expectations for the child.

When conflicts between teacher and child arise, parents should avoid the impulse to protect their child by immediately taking his or her side. A healthier approach is to work through the problem with discussions among the teacher, child, and parents. This procedure helps the child to understand that parents value both the teacher's and his or her views.

A single child's friends. In the early school years, friends take on a new importance to a single child. Friends not only alleviate loneliness and feelings of isolation, they also help the single child develop a more realistic perspective of him- or herself. Parents of single children firmly believe that it is important to encourage the single child not only to have friends but to prize them.

"One value I worked hard to instill in my daughter was the importance of friends," said the mother of an adult single child. "I taught her that friends were not people to use but people to give to and share with. I think it's paid off. My daughter has a friend who's as close to her as any sister could be."

Based on the studies discussed in Chapter 2 suggesting that single children's intellectual development is negatively affected by the lack of sibling teaching experience,[6] it would seem helpful for parents to encourage their single child to spend some time with younger children. Although not precisely duplicating the experience of having a younger sibling, the time spent with younger children will allow the single child to practice the skills of explanation, demonstration, and instruction, which are important to his or her own intellectual growth.

Parents' attitudes toward their child's friends. Setting high standards for their own child, parents of a single child often consciously or unconsciously place the same demands on their child's friends. "In eighteen years of living at home," remembered one single child, "my parents never approved of a single friend I brought home. Either the person was too rich or too poor, too unattractive or too concerned about appearances, too dumb or too booky. It's a wonder I ever had any friends the way my parents treated them."

Unless parents feel strongly that a particular friend is an unhealthy influence, they need to let their child choose his or her own friends and work out relationships with them. The experience is crucial for the child's understanding of the world beyond his or her home and parents.

Peer problems. Although parents should give their child reasonable freedom in working out individual friendships, they should be alert to the child's general peer relationships. Some signs of problems, or potential problems, between the single child and his or her peers include:

1. Always having friends considerably older or younger in age.
2. Never having a best friend.
3. Never having a friend for more than a few days.
4. Declining to get involved in extracurricular activities.
5. Attempting to "buy" friends with gifts.
6. Associating only with "lower status" children, such as school dropouts and troublemakers.
7. Being constantly at odds with peers.
8. Having friends of only one sex.[7]

Parents who observe these behaviors in their child need
not panic, but they should continue to observe their child's
interaction with friends to determine if he or she is having
trouble relating to peers.

"I want a brother or sister" requests. As the single child becomes
familiar with other children's families, he or she begins to
express a desire to have a sibling. The desire is especially
high in the first and second grades, when other children may
be reporting the arrival of new brothers and sisters.

How should parents respond to their child's questions
about a sibling? "Honestly," say experienced parents. Using a
positive approach, parents should explain that they love and
enjoy their child and do not want to interrupt that good
relationship by having another youngster. If there are financial considerations, those should be discussed, as should concerns about having the time or energy for another child. In
general, parents should emphasize benefits for the child,
while responding indirectly to the child's stated or unstated
fear that his or her parents are not having another child
because they are unhappy with him or her. Finally, parents
should convey to the child that family size is a decision parents must make because they are responsible for the welfare
of the family unit.

Family decision-making. Although there are certain decisions,
such as having another child, that must be made exclusively
by parents, it is important that the single child be allowed to
participate frequently in family decision-making. Not only
will the child receive valuable experience in making decisions, but having a voice in family affairs keeps the child
from feeling that the family odds are always stacked against
him or her. A voice in decisions about family activities (where
to go on vacation, who to have as guests in the home, where
to dine out, and so on) and about division of labor in the
household are especially important, as illustrated by Karen's
experience.

"When Calvin started school," explained Karen, "we began to assign him certain tasks around the house—emptying the trash or sweeping the porch, for example. He griped about doing those things, saying it was unfair because he didn't have anyone to share the chores with. Finally we started giving him a list of things that needed to be done and letting him choose a certain number to do. We also added a small payment for some of the jobs so he would see there was a payoff. Just giving him a voice in the decision and a money reward made a big difference in his attitude."

Keeping the child out of parents' conflicts. Involving the single child in many family decisions is healthy, but when it comes to the parents' marital or interpersonal problems, the child should never be purposely involved. Jackson, a college-age single child, described his early home life.

"My parents developed serious marital problems while I was still in elementary school. In a well-intentioned effort to be 'honest' with me, each of them would individually tell me what they thought was wrong with the other one. Their 'honesty' left me completely incapacitated. I loved them both, but as a child I was incapable of helping them with their adult problems. I could only anguish about them."

In a small unit like the one-child family, a child will be aware of and sensitive to adult problems, and parents should confirm the child's suspicions by acknowledging that there are problems. Having acknowledged the problems, parents should then make it clear that their difficulties are not caused by the child, that they are trying to work them out, and that he or she is not responsible for trying to find a solution.

Travel. "My best advice to parents of onlies," reflected Gladys, the mother of one adult child, "is always to take another child along when you go someplace. Children see things differently than adults, and they have more fun when they have experiences together. Besides, they entertain each other and give parents a chance to enjoy things in their own way."

Whether going for a two-hour trip to the zoo or a two-week vacation, parents of single children believe that the whole family is better off when their child takes along a friend.

Overnight visits and camp. One way in which a child begins to establish independence from parents is to spend nights away from them. Both overnight visits with relatives or friends and longer camp experiences are important—for child and parents. Not only do they help to break dependency patterns, but they also expose the child to different living routines.

"The first time I stayed overnight with a friend, I couldn't believe all the things her mother did 'wrong,'" laughed Bette. "We didn't even have to brush our teeth before going to bed. It was the first time I realized that maybe everybody didn't live just like my family did."

Solo visits by the single child also mediate a child's dismay at sometimes being left out of parents' activities. When the child begins to have a life independent of parents, their separate activities do not seem so "unfair."

Extending the family. Perhaps the greatest need of the school-age single child is to develop a secure, healthy sense of family. Because the child will be coping with being "different" by not having brothers or sisters, it is essential that his or her need for family identification be recognized. Parents of single children suggest two ways to meet this need.

One is to increase the child's involvement with his or her extended biological family. "My husband and I hadn't had much contact with our aunts and uncles before our daughter was born," explained Peg, "but when we realized how important having a 'family' was to her, we began to make an effort to be with relatives on holidays and vacations. Having cousins she knew well—even though we didn't live close—gave Kathy the feeling of being involved in a larger family."

A second approach suggested by parents is to extend the concept of "family" to include friends as well as relatives "When Denise was growing up," remarked a one-child mother, "we 'adopted' another family who had a single daughter just her age. The six of us became very close friends and spent lots of time together. We even had an agreement whereby Denise would spend one Saturday night and Sunday morning with our friends, then their daughter would spend the next weekend with us. The girls loved it, and the arrangement gave us adults a mini-vacation every other week."

Moving toward Adolescence

The single child begins the school years with his or her world revolving mainly around home and parents. By the time adolescence is reached, the child's world includes peers, school activities, away-from-home experiences, and ties with an extended family. With this foundation, the child plunges, headlong, into adolescence.

The Adolescent Years (Ages 12–18)

After having a special need for family in the early school years, the single child seems to lose the need for family in the adolescent years. Modeling his or her friends, the teen-age single child appears to live only for the approval of peers, and parents become verbal sparring partners.

Many one-child parents believe that single children tend to measure themselves against adults more than other teen-agers. Perhaps because the single child has a special need to receive adult approval, perhaps because there is no peer in the home, the teen-age single child tends to identify him- or herself in adult terms—a situation that can make adolescence a particularly frustrating time.

The main thrust of the teen-ager's energy is independence. Like other young people, teen-age single children must establish their self-sufficiency in thinking, personal life-style, money management, sexual development, and choice of friends. However, because they continue to confront the "only child" stigma, single children may feel an even stronger need to demonstrate independence than other teens.

Special Rearing Needs

When asked how to rear a teen-age single child, one father replied, "with fear and trembling." In reality, the single child's needs are much the same as other teens, with special considerations being mostly a matter of degree.

Importance of peers in adolescence. To teen-agers, friends are not just important, they are *everything*. Child development specialists believe that peers are critical in the healthy development of adolescents. A teen-ager's friend serves as a teacher, helps the teen achieve independence from family, affords opportunities to acquire sex information, and provides a source of status and prestige.[8]

For the child without siblings, the peer role becomes especially important. Rather than being disturbed by their child's involvement with or devotion to friends, parents should welcome the time their child spends with peers. Parents should only become concerned if their teen-ager does not establish peer relationships.

Other adult models. "As a teen-ager, my daughter worshiped her friend's mother," said one mother of an adult single child. "Frankly I was hurt because the woman was, in my view, rather crass and certainly not the kind of woman I wanted my daughter emulating."

Many one-child parents observe that their teen-age child

seems to emulate or develop a special fondness for another adult. Often the adult is a teacher or relative, but it also can be someone only slightly known to parents. In most cases the child's interest in the adult is another effort to extend his or her knowledge of other people by analyzing "up close" the behavior of an adult other than parents. By doing this, he or she identifies more options for his or her own life-style.

Relations with parents. The experiences of parents who have reared a single child through adolescence vary. Some parents report, "I think we had an easier time because we had such a close relationship with our child." Others say, "Our child's teen years were a powder keg because there was no other child in the household to moderate the parent-child tension." Still others feel that their experience was no better or worse than other families'.

Because the one-child family unit fosters togetherness, it is likely that parents and their adolescent child will have a closer than average relationship. The parenting question is how to make that closeness a positive influence during the child's adolescence. Experienced parents advise:

1. View your child's friends in positive terms. Being jealous is unproductive since your child can have close friends and still be close to you.

2. Remember that although the teen-ager is not a child, he or she is not yet an adult either. Don't involve your child in adult discussions or adult decisions that are beyond his or her level of maturity.

3. Avoid being manipulated by your teen-age single child. Teen-agers are especially fond of the line, "You've deprived me because you didn't provide me siblings." Parents say that this declaration is the single child's ultimate manipulation.

Fostering independent decision-making. "You want to let them make decisions," said Fred, the father of one, "but it's hard to sit back and let them make mistakes."

For parents and teen-agers, life seems to be a continuous series of decisions—most potential sources of conflict. Dating, driving, drugs, chores, part-time jobs, extracurricular activities, and movies are all issues that come up for discussion.

In confronting many of these questions, one-child parents believe that perspective is important. "Our kid hit us with 'everybody's doing it' every time she wanted something," Fred said later in the interview. "Without other kids in the house, we really weren't aware of what other teen-agers were doing, so we started making it a practice to find out. Not that we always let our daughter do everything everyone else was doing. But we tried to keep her in the mainstream of what was acceptable in her group of friends."

As for money decisions, parents agree that it is important for the single child to develop an appreciation of money. "It's hard to keep from overindulging an only child," believes one mother. "But it's important that the child have a sense of where that money comes from and what has to be done to get it."

Parents like this mother strongly advocate that the single child have a regular source of income (either an allowance or money from a job) and spend from that income. Not only does such spending instill a better sense of the value of money, it also allows the child to become somewhat financially independent of parents.

Crises. At every age level, crises seem to hit the single child a little harder than children with siblings. When traumas such as death, divorce, or serious illness strike, parents tend to relate to each other and the adult aspects of the situation, while the single child is left without a colleague to share the tension and uncertainty.

Parents who have experienced such crises avow the importance of providing a source of support for the child during such times—whether it be another child or an adult. Recalling the day her husband died, one mother said, "About 6:00 p.m. the evening his father died, Ken came to me and asked if he could spend the night with Charlie, his best friend. I was shocked and hurt because I thought he was running out on me. I burst into tears, and he stayed home.

"I've regretted that decision ever since," continued the mother, "because it was selfish of me. I had my sister and mother there to comfort me, but Ken really had no one his own age to talk with."

From Adolescence to Adulthood

Whether a child is a single or has several siblings, the transition from adolescence to adulthood is never painless. However, if one-child parents use the opportunity of their small family to develop a close relationship with their child and allow the child a true voice in the family decision-making, the family can emerge from the adolescent years without major battle scars and eager to enjoy the child's adulthood.

seven / *The Single Child as an Adult*

> Being an only *child* is of small consequence. Being an *adult* only is of large consequence.
>
> A SINGLE CHILD, AGE 45

Whether their road to maturity is rocky or smooth, single children become adults. Just as brothers and sisters must leave the security of home and venture out into the world, so must single children. What happens to single children in adulthood? What happens to parents after their "only chick" leaves the nest? Are the consequences of singleness really more profound in adulthood than in childhood?

After High School

Graduation from high school usually marks a period of transition for parents and child. Often the child leaves home to live independently. Even if he or she stays at home, there is generally a marked decline in the amount of control that parents attempt to exercise over the child—and the amount of control a child will accept from parents.

After graduation, single children face the same decisions

as other young adults. Some go to work, some get married, some continue to "live off their parents," and some go to college.

College

"It was always assumed I would go to college," said Maxine in an interview. "Since my parents had only one child, they could afford to send me to college. They wanted me to have every opportunity in life, and I wanted to go, so there was no reason not to."

Eighty-seven per cent of the single children in our study reported some college experience. This is a high percentage of college attendance when compared to figures showing that today 58 per cent of all high school graduates enroll in college (a decade ago 33 per cent enrolled).[1] Of those in our study who started college, 50 per cent had completed their degree (13 per cent were still in college); 28 per cent had done graduate work beyond the bachelor level (Appendix 1). Previous studies have also demonstrated that more single children expect to enroll in college, receive a degree, and pursue graduate work than children from any other family size.[2]

Many single children feel that they "shed the cloak of singleness" for the first time when they get to college. Clarice, a college student, remarked, "When I lived at home in a small midwestern community, I always felt people expected too much, or too little, from me because they knew I was an only child. Since I've come to college, nobody really knows or cares that I'm an only, so I've stopped being so self-conscious about it."

In her studies with college students at Wake Forest University and the Center of Creative Leadership in Greensboro, North Carolina, Dr. Toni Falbo found the single children no lonelier, no more neurotic or unhappy than their college classmates who had siblings. However, the single children were somewhat more independent, trusting, and likely to be leaders.[3] Parents will be pleased to note that single children in another study put in 50 per cent more study hours than their college classmates who had siblings.[4]

Noncollege Experiences

The single children in our study who had not gone to college were following fairly typical life patterns. Several young men had gone into family businesses after high school. The single daughters had married or taken jobs. Only two of the adult singles were living with their parents.

Making the Break

Whether the single child goes to college or takes a job after high school, it is important that a physical break from parents be made sometime in the child's late teens or early twenties. If the break does not come at this "natural" time in the child's life, parents and child may find the break more difficult, or perhaps impossible, later.

The difficulty of making the break from home depends on how much independence parents have encouraged in their child. Two stories illustrate opposite experiences.

Jan's story:
My first night in the college dorm was the first time I had spent the night away from my parents. I'd never even stayed overnight with a friend.

Needless to say, the separation anxiety was tremendous for both my parents and me. I think I called them or they called me every day for two months. I didn't know how to manage my own life. I'd never written a check or washed my own clothes. I'd never even set my own hair—mother always did it.

I ended up dropping out of school after one semester. It wasn't that my grades were bad; I just couldn't cope with having to manage on my own. Unfortunately, my parents didn't encourage me to stay in school. They missed me and wanted me home.

I went back home and lived with my parents for the next three years, until I got married and moved—three blocks away. I still see my parents every day, sometimes twice a day. I guess you might say I still haven't left home—and I'm 37 years old.

Shirley's story:

I honestly don't remember many problems when I left home. My parents had been preparing me to be independent for years. I'd gone to some kind of camp every summer from junior high through high school, so I was used to being away from my folks. I had a checking account when I was a high school freshman. It didn't have much in it, but I learned to write checks and balance my checkbook. I worked at the local drugstore two nights a week during my senior year, so I had some money of my own. Because my mother worked, I learned how to cook and do my laundry.

I think my folks were disappointed when I chose to take a job in another city rather than go to college after high school, but they wished me well and didn't try to con me into changing my plans. Now I see them once a year or so. They always say how they wish I lived closer, but they never pressure me to come back to the hometown, and I love them for that.

Careers

"I've never really thought about whether being an only child has influenced my professional career," said Rachael, a medical researcher, "but I suppose it has. For one thing, I purposely chose to go into research rather than a medical practice because I don't like being with people constantly. Also, I am able to spend longer periods of time in the lab than other people, and that probably goes back to spending more time by myself as a child."

As Rachael's comments suggest, the childhood experiences of single children seem to have a bearing on both their career choice and their career success.

Career Choices

Although single children can be found in an array of professions, they seem to gravitate toward certain areas. For example, studies show a large percentage of scientists and scholars are firstborn or single children.[5] For single children the choice seems natural. Because they spend more time by themselves as children, single-child adults are better able to tolerate long periods of isolated work. They also tend to be more resourceful in seeking solutions to problems, and their need to achieve makes them willing to expend the time and energy necessary for exacting work.

A vivid example of single children's inclination toward scientific careers arose during the American astronaut program in the late 1960s. Of the 23 astronauts who traveled in space during that time, 21 were firstborns or single children. Number of siblings was not a consideration in the selection of astronauts, but psychologists speculated that characteristics which were sought—self-reliance, ability to tolerate loneliness, and setting high standards for oneself—were most likely to be found in firstborn or single children.[6]

Single children are also attracted to other professions. Professor Joseph Mancuso, author of numerous books on the successful entrepreneur, says that an overwhelming majority of successful people who start and manage their own businesses are also firstborn or single children. An unusually high percentage of applicants to medical, dental, law, and pharmacy schools are single children.[7] Undoubtedly, the high value placed on achievement in one-child families leads single children into "high status" professions. Probably the ability of one-child parents to afford the extended education needed for these professions is also a factor.

Dr. Lucille Forer believes that because of their early independence and self-reliance, single children are often attracted into the political arena.[8] Some well-known single children in politics include Franklin Roosevelt, Joseph Stalin, and Indira Gandhi.

Of the single-child adults in our study, 28 per cent were engaged in professional careers, including education, medicine, engineering, science, and law (Appendix 1). Most reported being happy with their career choices and felt that being a single child had helped them to pursue a vocation of interest to them.

Career Success

From their case studies of single children, Cutts and Moseley concluded that the vocational success of single children was comparable to that of nonsingles.[9] Certainly there are examples of single children who have excelled in a variety of career fields, such as:

Hans Christian Andersen—Danish fairy tale writer

Mary Astor—actress

Frank Borman—astronaut

Antonia Brico—symphony conductor

Buddha—religious philosopher and teacher

Kenneth Clark—art historian and author

Sammy Davis, Jr.—entertainer

Albert Einstein—physicist, musician, humanitarian

Edsel Ford—industrialist

Betty Furness—television personality

Indira Gandhi—Prime Minister of India

William Randolph Hearst—newspaper publisher

Charles Evans Hughes—Chief Justice of the United States Supreme Court

Shirley Jones—actress

Leonardo da Vinci—artist and inventor

Charles Lindbergh—aviator

James A. Lovell—astronaut

Mary, Queen of Scots—ruler of Scotland

Marilyn Monroe—actress

Eleanor Roosevelt—humanitarian

Franklin Roosevelt—president of the United States

Jean-Paul Sartre—philosopher and writer

Roger Stauback—football quarterback

Joseph Stalin—Soviet dictator

Robert Louis Stevenson—Scottish author

Margaret Truman—author

Queen Victoria—British monarch

Oscar Wilde—writer

The single child's need to succeed may be primarily responsible for his or her vocational success. Single children's parents generally place a high value on success, and single children strive to live up to that expectation. A good education and often financial help to get started in a career help to insure that goals are met.

Preparing the Single Child for a Career

Consciously or unconsciously, parents influence a child's career attitudes throughout childhood. The work habits they develop in the child will carry over into his or her job. The attitudes toward work that the parents convey to the child—work is pleasure, work is drudgery—help to determine the child's on-the-job attitudes. The value that parents attach to work and achievement will make vocational success more—or less—important to the child.

Beyond attitudes and habits, one-child parents should make a special effort to expose their child to a wide variety of career options and avoid pressuring the child into a particular career. Having put "all their eggs in one basket," single-child parents are often very determined that their child enter medicine or science—or some other profession they see as high status. Recognizing that he or she is solely responsible for fulfilling parents' expectations, a single child feels more pressure to go into the vocation of his or her parents' choice. But that pressure can be anguishing, as in the following case of Thomas, an aspiring young actor.

My father is the director of a bank in surburban Chicago. For as long as I can remember my father has said, "When Thomas takes over the bank, I will do so and so." When I was a little kid, I thought that would be okay. But by the time I got to high school I realized that I didn't have the abilities needed in banking—I was lousy at math, hated meetings, and thought worrying about money was boring.

When I went to college, I started in a prebusiness curriculum, not because I wanted to, but because dad wanted me to. My roomate that first year was a drama major, and I started hanging around the theater. It soon became clear that I was much more interested in acting than banking—and that I was much better at it.

In the summer before my junior year, I decided to tell dad I was changing majors. It took me a summer to work up the courage. When I finally told him, he came unglued. After a lot of comments about how unimportant acting was and how I would never get anywhere in the theater, he threw in the final shot: "You know you're our only child. If you don't come into the bank with me, it will be lost to our family. Is that fair to your mother and me?"

I went ahead and graduated with a degree in drama and have hopes of becoming a successful actor someday. I hope my father will find some pleasure in my success when and if it comes.

Once their child is into a career, parents should avoid voicing discontent about his or her job choice or achievement. Adult single children in our study felt that they carried a heavy burden in trying to fulfill their parents' aspirations, especially when they were constantly reminded that because they were a single child, they were solely responsible for "making parents proud."

Rita, a young woman who recently completed a Ph.D. in chemistry, recalled: "No matter how hard I try or how much I accomplish, it never seems enough for my parents. I thought maybe getting the doctorate would do it, but no.

Right after commencement my mother said to me, 'Now if you can just write a book.' Their expectations are insatiable."

Marriage

"Getting married was very exciting for me because it was the first time I had a chance to experience a close companionship with someone my own age," reported a recent single-child bride.

Like this bride, most single children when they marry experience their first intimate, continuing relationship with a person other than parents. Some single children in our study said that they saw their spouse, in part, as the sibling they didn't have in childhood.

There is little research to indicate how single children fare as marriage partners. In the 1930s two research projects studied the marital happiness of couples and concluded that the marital happiness of couples in which one or both partners were single children[10] was about the same as that of other couples. One of the research teams suggested that it was difficult to pinpoint onliness as a determining factor of marital happiness since so many other factors such as personality and parental attachment also must be considered.[11] From his observations, Dr. Murray Kappelman concluded that while the single child may have to learn to compromise more in marriage than he or she has been accustomed to, the "only child can make a superb marriage partner. . . . The ability to have the other person so close after long years of aloneness often makes the only child an eager, caring, almost overly solicitious mate."[12]

Marriage from a Single Child's Viewpoint

When asked if being an only child affected their marital relationships, the majority (59 per cent) of our respondents said "no" (Appendix 1). "Whatever effects onliness had on me in

childhood had disappeared by the time I was ready to marry"
was the common sentiment of those answering in the negative.

Of the 41 per cent who felt that their singleness had affected their marriages, some named negative effects:

> Difficult to share and compromise.
> I'm torn between my spouse and my parents.
> I expect too much attention.
> I set unrealistic expectations for my spouse.
> I need the house very quiet.
> I need more independence than he or she is willing to give.
> I don't like the responsibilities involved in marriage.
> Not having a sibling, it's hard to put my spouse's behavior in perspec-
> tive.
> I am jealous of my spouse's family ties.
> I need more privacy than my spouse.

Others thought the effects had been positive:

> I feel I am closer to my spouse.
> I value my spouse more.
> I turn to my spouse as a helpmate in overcoming problems.
> I enjoy and value companionship with my spouse.
> I enjoy my spouse's family more.
> My spouse is better accepted by my parents.

The wide variety of responses suggests that the effect of
singleness in marriage is very individual. The experiences
described by our subjects make it clear that singleness does
not predict how single children will act as marriage partners.

Parents and Their Single Child's Marriage

'I was very concerned because our son didn't marry until he
was thirty-five," reported one mother. "His father and I are
both getting up in years, and we feel better knowing that he

will have his own family when we are gone." Contrary to popular belief, most parents of single children were pleased when their child married. Parents saw their child's marriage as a continuing source of companionship for him or her after they died.

What role do parents play in the marital experience of their child (or children)? The most profound influence comes from the example they set as marriage partners. Although all children model their own parents, the intensity and closeness of the one-child family focuses the single child's attention on his or her parents even more closely. The best way, then, to prepare a single child, or any child, for a successful marriage is for parents to have a happy marriage themselves.

Once a child is married, the healthiest role parents can play is that which encourages the continued independence of their child from them. "If it doesn't work out, you can always come home" is a counterproductive contingency for parents to offer their child. Of course, parents will continue to love and care about their child, but a policy of noninterference in the child's relationship with his or her spouse is especially important for one-child parents because of their tendency to overfocus on their child.

It is particularly critical that parents avoid criticizing or setting expectations for their child's spouse. One-child parents, accustomed to having their son or daughter seek their approval, tend to expect the same from their in-law. But one mother's experience illustrates the predictable result.

"I am an immaculate housekeeper," confided Mable, "and I taught Lawrence to value tidiness—at least I thought I did. He married a girl who is a nice, talented person, but their house is an absolute disaster. The first time we went to visit them I was so appalled I started to tidy up. Lawrence's wife threw a fit and let me know that she didn't need or want my help. In the midst of the tirade, my son took me aside and said, 'Mother, when I lived at home I always tried to be neat because you made me and because I knew it was important to you. But now I live with Joanne and she doesn't care about having the house spotless, and, truthfully, neither do I. So you'll just have to accept the place the way it is or not come back.' I realized from that little speech that I no longer had the last word with him."

For parents concerned about the effect of the one-child family on their child's chances for marital success, Dr. Eda LeShan makes this observation: "Just as in every other aspect of growing up, readiness for marriage and parenthood will have a lot more to do with the basic attitudes of parents, together with the life experiences of the family members, than with the fact of being an only child."[13]

Single Children as Parents

"I remember when I was about six years old," said an adult single child, "I would tell my mother that when I grew up I was going to have ten kids so I would have somebody to play with. Fortunately I realized it doesn't work that way before I started my own family."

Many single children remember making some rather definite statements in childhood about what size family they would have or how they would rear their children. What they actually do as parents is often different from their predictions.

Size of Family

A commonly held belief in our society is that single children are unhappy with their own childhood experiences and they compensate by having larger than average families themselves. Studies suggest that this is not true. The single children whom Cutts and Moseley studied in the 1950s had smaller than average families,[14] and parents in our study showed the same tendency. Among our single-child respondents who were parents (and reported their family complete), 70 per cent had one or two children (Appendix 1). Of the adults who were not yet parents, 62 per cent said that they would like to have one or two children.

Do single children have one-child families themselves? Among our respondents, 21 per cent who reported their families complete had a single child. In the general population, only 10 per cent of all parents have one child, so the number of single children in our study having single children was about twice what would be expected.[15]

Because the number of respondents in our study was limited, it is impossible to generalize about family size preferences of single children. However, it appears that single children tend to conform to the general American trend to have small families, but they do not tend to repeat their own family experience by having a single child.

Parenting from a Single Child's Viewpoint

"I don't think being an only child has affected me much as a wife, but it certainly affects me as a mother," reflected Faye. Other single children who are parents tend to agree. Although only 41 per cent of our adult subjects felt that singleness affected them in marriage, 61 per cent felt that it affected their parenting (Appendix 1). A wide range of effects, both positive and negative, were mentioned.

Positive effects on parenting:

I allow my children more independence.

We have more open communication.

I enjoy the relationship among my children.

I try to avoid being demanding.

I value my children more.

I spend more time with them.

I'm inclined to try to channel their interests as my parents did mine.

I stress sharing.

As an only child, I understand my only child.

Negative effects on parenting:

Sibling bickering makes me nervous.

It's hard to put my kids first.

I miss a quiet life.

I spoil my own children.

I'm too demanding.

I don't like to participate in children's activities.

Communicating with my children about sex is difficult.

Of the many effects suggested by single children who are parents, the most commonly mentioned (and the one that seemed most distressing) was an inability to cope with the bickering of their own children. Part of the explanation undoubtedly lies in the fact that single children generally grow up in relatively quiet homes and simply do not experience the arguing and physical competition found in multichild families. But one mother of three suggested a more deepseated reason.

"During my childhood I had a very idealized vision of what it would be like to have a brother or sister," said this mother. "I imagined we would have wonderful long talks, share our toys and clothes, and go places together. When I had my own children, I fully expected them to have this kind of relationship. Instead, they constantly bicker and pick at each other. Other people tell me it's normal, but it gets on my nerves and it really disappoints me."

Despite difficulty in accepting the noise and bickering of their children, most single children enjoy being parents. Many believe they take more delight in their children than people who have had siblings because the multichild family experience is new to them. "Other parents take children's relationships for granted," said one father, "but I'm fascinated by them and get a great kick out of seeing my kids relate to each other."

Single Children and Their Aging Parents

As we concluded an interview, Edith, a single child in her early sixties, added this postscript:

> If you had asked me ten years ago what I thought about being an only child, I would have said it's fine. My parents and I always got along exceptionally well, and I thought I was lucky to be an only.
>
> But I feel differently about it now. Several years ago my father became ill, and I spent long hours helping my mother care for him until he died. He had barely been gone six months when my mother had a stroke. She was in the hospital for a month before we brought her to our home for a few months. Now she's in a nursing home. Since her resources are almost exhausted, I not only have the emotional responsibility for her care but the financial responsibility as well. I really wish I had a brother or sister to share this load.

Edith was not alone in her concern and frustration. Many adult single children mentioned "having sole responsibility for the care of parents" as an important disadvantage of being a single child.

Parents' Retirement

In the life cycle of most one-child families, the relationship between parents and their child is most independent and calm after the child marries and has a family. That calm is often abruptly broken when parents reach retirement. "The day my dad retired, it became a new ball game," according to one single daughter.

Problems seem to occur when the retiring parents, suddenly having time on their hands, look to their child to fill the void. One set of parents moved from their lifelong home in the East to the mountains of Wyoming to be near their only daughter. Another father started "visiting" his son's printing business every day. In one case, a single daughter started using her recently retired parents as almost full-time babysitters.

There is nothing inherently wrong or inappropriate with any of these situations if all persons involved are agreeable. But the parents who moved to Wyoming were unhappy because they had no friends, and their daughter became frustrated with their lack of interest in anything except her and her family. The son resented his father meddling in his business—a business the son had begun in order to avoid going into his father's dry cleaning store. And the grandparents resented being tied down with their grandchildren, but they were reluctant to say anything for fear of being misinterpreted.

Retirement need not be a time of difficulty, but some pre-retirement planning is necessary. Families who handle the retirement period best are ones in which parents and child have a frank discussion before retirement of what parents will do and how the child will be involved. If a major life change, such as a move, is planned, parents may want to "test run" the change to see if it is the best choice for them and their child.

Physical Incapacity

Caring for parents who become ill or physically incapacitated concerns all children, but the responsibility falls particularly hard on the single child who has no one with whom to share the load. Single children who have confronted this problem handled it in a variety of ways. One woman gave up her career, moved in with her parents, and took care of them until their deaths. Others took their parents into their homes or arranged care in a nursing home.

There is really no "good" solution to the problem of caring

for physically or mentally incapacitated parents, but, again, preplanning can help. While parents are still able, they should discuss possible eventualities with their child and draw up a mutually agreeable plan. Later circumstances may force modifications, but a single child will feel less overwhelmed by the responsibility if he or she feels that parents' wishes are being followed.

Financial Responsibility

The physical care of aging parents is often coupled with a responsibility to provide financial support. No matter what the financial status of parents, there should be joint financial planning by parents and child so that the child does not have to bear the brunt of financial support for parents.

Death

"I've always tried to compensate for whatever problems my son might encounter as an only child," said a one-child parent, age 70. "But I can't do much for him after I'm dead, now can I?"

As one-child parents grow older, they frequently worry about what will happen to their child after they die. They worry about not being around to "provide" for their child, and they worry about the son or daughter having to face their death without brothers and sisters for support. Single children also worry about their parents' deaths, dreading the "lack of family" that will result.

The legal and financial problems surrounding parents' deaths can be eased by preplanning about burial arrangements, property dispersion, and will probation. However, the emotional trauma of parents' deaths and the resulting loss of family relationship simply must be dealt with as one reality of being a single child.

Preparing for the Future—Parents and Child

Many adult single children feel that the most serious disadvantage of singleness is the sole responsibility for parents in later years. The responsibility is a fact of life for a single child and should not be taken lightly by either child or parents. Nevertheless, single children can take comfort in recognizing that having a brother or sister is not always the answer to the problem of aging parents. There are many multichild families in which one child assumes, either by choice or default of other siblings, the total responsibility for parents. The answer to the problem of caring for aging parents is not having siblings; it is advance planning by parents and child for the parents' last years.

The following suggestions can help parents to minimize problems in their later years.

1. Encourage or insist that your child make the break from home in young adulthood. Caring for elderly parents is easier if the child has established his or her independence in earlier years.
2. Establish your own independence. Build your personal life and your married life so that you do not depend on your child for your happiness or your interest in living.
3. If possible, build your financial resources so that your child does not have the financial burden of your last years.
4. Insist on serious, detailed planning with your child about your financial resources and how you are to be cared for should you become incapacitated.
5. Ease the trauma of your death for your child by leaving your financial matters in order and making your funeral/burial wishes known.

Single Children in Later Years

Pauline is a single child now in her early sixties. "When I was younger," she says, "I could never understand the expression 'the lonely only child.' As a child I had lots of friends and a very busy life. At college I met new people and had more to do than I could keep up with. I married in my late twenties, had two children, and of course they occupied me for the next twenty years or so. Then things began to change. My son and daughter married and moved out of state, my father died, then a few years later my mother passed away. Now for the first time in my life I feel very lonely. I still have many friends and keep busy with social activities, but I feel a great lack of family. The thought of losing my husband really frightens me."

Most single children in their fifties and sixties agree with Pauline that they suffer more "loneliness" in their later years than when they're younger. In childhood their parents are with them; in early and middle adulthood their own children occupy them. But when children begin to leave the household and parents pass away, single children have only their spouse, or in the case of unmarried persons, no close family member. Their "loneliness" results not so much from the absense of persons in their lives, because they often have many friends, but from a deep-felt sense of missing the family companionship of brothers and sisters.

In elaborating on their feeling of loneliness, some of the older respondents speculated on what their life would be like if they had a sibling to share their older years. For example, Heddy, an engaging, "sixtyish" woman said, "I often think, 'Oh, if I just had a sister, someone I could talk over my problems with, someone who could share my worries about growing old, about my kids, my husband, just everything.' I think no two people can be closer than sisters."

The picture Heddy has painted of having a sister is an ideal—an ideal that is often not met in real-life sibling relationships. She, and other single children, seldom consider that a sibling might live thousands of miles away, have no common interests, engage them in an estate dispute, or genuinely dislike them.

Although regret about lack of siblings cannot be eliminated in later years, there are characteristics that, if developed in younger years, will help a single child to be less remorseful in older age. To develop these characteristics in their child, parents can:

1. Help their child to develop skills of relating to people in meaningful ways. Encourage close friends, people to whom the child can turn in times of joy and sorrow.

2. Help their child to develop a variety of interests in life. Hobbies and avocations help to fill time, but, more important, they bring people into contact with others who share common interests.

3. Teach their child to value friends. A single child will not have "built-in" family for companionship, but good friends can help to fill this void. "I think close friends are even closer than siblings," theorized an adult single child. "Siblings just happen to be born into the same family, but you choose your friends."

Singleness: The Single Child's Perspective

Throughout this book we have presented single children's thoughts on being a single child. The diversity of opinions and experiences related by the subjects is so broad that it defies a definition of a "typical single child" or a "single-child syndrome." However, there is a commonality of general experiences discussed by the single children in our study. By combining descriptions of these experiences, it is possible to suggest what it is like to be a single child—from a single child's point-of-view.

In childhood, single children do not believe that they are very different from their peers. They sometimes feel lonely but are glad to miss sibling rivalry and competition. Their childhood problems are not very different from those of their friends, except that they don't have sibling frustrations. They sometimes have other single children as best friends, but not usually. Single children do not think other children are very aware of their singleness or that it makes much difference to them.

Most single children wish for a brother or sister at certain times in their lives. Early school years are the most common time, but many would also like to have a sibling during adolescence and again in later adulthood. As a rule, single children receive more attention from their parents than other children, but they believe this attention is more beneficial than harmful. Their singleness draws them closer to their parents.

Those with experience believe that the effects of singleness do not stop with childhood, but the effects are very individual in adulthood. Although the majority of married single children do not believe that singleness affects their marital relationships, those who are parents think it does affect their parenting, in both positive and negative ways. Older single children feel more loneliness in their later years than in childhood. Having sole responsibility for the care of aging parents weighs heavily on them.

Few single children see their experience as black or white. Instead they view singleness as a mixture of advantages and disadvantages, which tend to balance each other. Across the board, single children believe that their parents' approach to rearing was more important in their development than the fact that they had no sibling. "If parents are okay, onliness is okay," declared one interviewee.

Single children acknowledge that being a single child has been important in their life experience, but many feel that the effects are overrated. One college student, a young man who had given much thought to being a single child, summarized his feelings this way: "I am the kind of person I am partly because I'm an only child. But I'm also who I am because I was born in a small town, because my parents are middle class, because I am Catholic, because I have asthma, and because I am reasonably intelligent. I don't believe being an only child is really any more important than any of the other facts that have made me what I am."

eight / *Single Parent– Single Child*

You've got to concentrate on what your child has and stop worrying about what he or she is missing.

A SINGLE FATHER WHO IS
REARING A SINGLE CHILD

Since her divorce five years ago, Jill has had the primary responsibility for rearing her 10-year-old daughter, Cindy. "I guess you'd say I have one child by circumstance rather than choice," commented Jill. "Because our marriage was shaky, I didn't want to have more children while I was still married, and since I've not remarried, having a second child hasn't been feasible. I'm not regretful about it. In fact, it is probably better to have just one child in my situation."

Today, 15 per cent of all children under age 18 are being reared in single-parent homes. Ninety-four per cent of these households are headed by the mother and the other six per cent by the father.[1] Data from the National Opinion Research Center show that approximately 20 per cent of all single parents (widowed and divorced) are rearing one child.[2]

In our study of one-child parents, 18 per cent were parents without partners—14 per cent mothers and four per cent fathers. For many of these parents, divorce or the death of a spouse had precluded their having more children. Although each situation was unique, the parents expressed similar beliefs and concerns about the single-parent/single-child situation.

Inside the Single-Parent/Single-Child Family

Maria has been divorced for three years and has custody of her 10-year-old son, Clint. Reflecting on her role as the single parent of a single child, Maria said, "For me the difficult part is trying to decide if my son's ups and downs are because he doesn't have a brother or sister, because his father isn't in the home, because he's tired of me, or because he's just in a bad mood."

Problems in the one-child/one-parent situation are often difficult to sort out because of the intensity in the family unit. The intensity inherent in the one-child, two-parent home magnifies when there is only one parent. Possible interactions are reduced from four to two. "Without a second parent," said one single mother, "there is no buffer—for either the child or the parent."

Single parents have mixed views on the overall effect of not having a second parent in the household. "My ex-wife and I had absolutely contradictory opinions on how our son should be reared," recalled Don, a single father. "When I got custody of Jay after the divorce, I relaxed because I knew that I could call the shots. Whether my judgment is good or bad, at least I don't have to argue with my ex-wife about it." The feeling of being in charge plus the press of multiple responsibilities can lead to a new perspective on parenting. Michael McFadden, in his book *Bachelor Fatherhood*, concludes that "single parents tend to be more relaxed about child-rearing simply because they don't have time to be any other way."[3]

Other parents don't agree that the single parent role is very relaxing. "I'm probably too hard on my child," confided a widowed mother whose only child is beginning adolescence. "I'm afraid that he'll mess up and people will say it's because he had neither father nor sibling. I know I need to loosen my control, but it's hard for me to know how much. I think it would be easier if I had his father to discuss it with."

For Kate, the mother of a two-year-old child, the problems of being a single parent are less philosophical and more a matter of time and energy. "I don't mind making decisions or providing for my daughter," said Kate, "but I get tired. Trying to work, take care of the house, pay the bills, have some kind of social life, and be a good mother overwhelms me."

Like his or her parent, the single child in a one-parent household feels the intensity of the situation. A child with only one parent cannot seek a "second opinion." "I respect my mother," said a 12-year-old single child, "but I truly believe that some of her decisions are wrong, and I have no court of appeals." Without that court of appeals, the in-home parent becomes the child's only continual source of feedback, criticism, support, and reward.

Dr. Murray Kappelman, author of *Raising the Only Child*, believes parent problems are compounded for the single child because he or she has "no forest of siblings into which he [she] can run and hide."[4] "If I had a sister," said a teen-age single child living with her mother, "at least I could gripe to her about mother. I talk to my friends about my disagreements with my mom, but they're not much help because they don't live with us and see what's going on."

Single children in one-parent homes often complain about the number of household tasks they are expected to assume. "My dad doesn't get home until 7:00 p.m.," explained the single daughter of a widowed father. "If I want to have something to eat, it's up to me to get dinner ready. I also do most of the laundry, because dad doesn't have time."

Some single parents acknowledge that they expect more household help from their child than do other parents. "My son is expected to keep his own room clean, dry the dishes every evening, keep the trash emptied, and vacuum once a week," explained a single mother. "That's more than the other ten-year-olds around us do, but I've got to have the help and I don't think it's hurting him." Jim and Janet Egleson, in their book *Parents Without Partners*, suggest that because of these kinds of experiences and responsibilities, "an only child may have to be more independent, and at an earlier age" than children with siblings in one-parent homes.[5]

A single parent and single child have perhaps the most intense, and potentially limiting, of all family situations. Without the balance and support of another adult, the single parent can easily fall prey to an unhealthy leniency or strictness in child-rearing. The single child, without the feedback of siblings or a second parent, can feel unfairly trapped in a situation not of his or her making and beyond his or her control. The potential for unhealthy consequences are real, but they don't have to happen. With attention to certain needs of both the parent and the child, the family unit can become rewarding and happy.

A Single Child's Needs

Every child needs assurance of love and stability, but for the single child who experiences a parent's death or the separation of parents the need for reassurance is particularly strong. The single child must absorb the shock of the crisis, and he or she must do it without the protective shield of siblings. The fears and anxieties common to all children during times of family instability are magnified for the single child who has no in-home peer to help him or her build confidence in the new family structure.

Relief from Fears

Although concerns of children who lose parents through divorce and those whose parents die are similar, there are somewhat different reactions and behavior in the two situations. One difference may be the child's initial reaction to the change in his or her family. In the case of divorce, the child's first response may be anger. "My child was furious when we told her we were going to separate," recalled a divorced mother. "She acted as if it were a frivolous decision on our part, and one which we would change if we truly cared about her."

Dr. Kappelman suggests that this reaction is typical. Even if the child has experienced serious tension and conflict in the home, Dr. Kappelman believes that the child "still wants an intact nuclear family, at any cost."[6] No doubt the thought of losing one-third of an already small family distresses the child. From the child's viewpoint, he or she is the sole unwilling victim of his or her parents' decision (they want it, he or she doesn't).

The advice of experts, as well as parents, is to try to soothe the child's fears by explaining, objectively, why the decision to separate has been made. Without name calling or going into elaborate detail, parents should tell the child that the problems are between them and in no way diminish their love for him or her. This message may have to be repeated again and again as the child attempts to convince him- or herself that he or she continues to be loved. "It's been two years since our divorce," commented a single mother, "and every once in a while my child still asks why daddy decided to live with another mommy."

Although divorce removes a parent from the child's day-to-day life, death removes a parent permanently and produces a different set of concerns. For a very young child, the mere concept of death is puzzling and frequently misunderstood. An older child may better understand the concept of death but be equally as perplexed about why this had to happen in his or her family.

Both younger and older children can develop fears after a parent's death. Many fear the loss of their remaining parent. "I was unaware of how insecure my son was after his mother's death," said a single father, "until his teacher told me he had talked to her about it. That night we had a chat, and I told him I was in good health and had no intentions of leaving him, but if something should happen to me, his grandparents would become his legal guardians. Just some straight talk about the situation seemed to relieve his anxiety."

Some children also begin to fear their own deaths after the loss of a parent. Jim and Janet Egleson write, "Quite naturally the death of a parent brings the specter of a child's own end closer to him [or her]. He has two major emotional problems: how to absorb the complete and final loss of his mother or his father, and how to ward off the threat that one day, he too, may cease to exist."[7] Again, the child needs help in confronting and dealing with this concern.

Whether the child has lost a parent through death or divorce, often he or she will have fears about the remaining parent's ability to provide care. "Will my mother (or father) be able to take care of me alone?" is a question asked by many children. Consulting psychologist Hanna E. Kapit suggests that even when the remaining parent displays self-confidence and optimism, the child "knowing that he [or she] used to have *two* parents, may feel insecure with only one parent."[8]

Only time and experience can actually convince the child that the parent is indeed up to the new responsibility, but some of the child's initial fears may be removed if parent and child talk out the concern. For example, if the child is old enough, a single mother might explain where their income will come from and how she will use it to provide for their needs. A single father might demonstrate that he can prepare a meal, or explain that he will hire a housekeeper to do the household tasks.

Single parents who confront fears in their single child should realize that such concerns are common to many children who live in one-parent families. However, they should also recognize that because their child has no immediate companions (brothers or sisters) to share fears, his or her anxieties may become magnified. To prevent such exaggerations, as well as to resolve other problems, many parents believe that a single child with a single parent needs an extended family or friendship network.

Extended Friendship Network

Here is the way a friendship network helped Flo, a part-time college student and mother of a six-year-old:

> Marsha was three when I was divorced. We nearly drove each other crazy that first year. She made enormous demands on me because her daddy was gone, and I tried to live up to all of them because I felt guilty about the divorce, which had been my idea. We spun a web around each other so tight we were both choking.
>
> About a year after the divorce I got into serious financial trouble and couldn't afford an apartment any longer. So Marsha and I moved into a big old house with two other single mothers and their kids. While we had some problems that year, I did learn the value of having more people for Marsha and me to interact with. I realized other people could fulfill certain needs in our lives and that we didn't have to be all things to each other.
>
> Since that experience we've lived several other places, but I've always looked for an apartment house or neighborhood where there are other single parents so that Marsha and I will have other kids and adults easily available to us as friends.

Many single parents in our study emphasized the importance of having an extended family or friendship network. Although most of them had not lived in a communal situation, they had taken special care to assure that their child had other children to play with on a continuing basis and other adults who could serve as role models for the child. The extended family and friend relationships also gave the parent needed companionship and emotional outlets. "You've got to meet the problem of too much intensity head on," said one father, "and the only way to do it is to get more people into your lives."

One important benefit of a single child's association with other adults is a better understanding of sex roles. Because the single parent plays dual roles of father and mother, the child picks up fewer traditional distinctions between what's "womanly" and what's "manly." Breaking down the sexual stereotypes is healthy, but the child does need exposure to adults opposite in sex from the in-home parent to help establish his or her own sexual identity.

"I was very aware of the importance of sex role learning in the home," said Laura, a child development specialist, "so when my husband and I split, I started doing all kinds of 'masculine' things with my son, like playing baseball and fixing his bike. Because I thought I was offering my child appropriate masculine encouragement, I was crushed one day when he announced that he wanted to go to a Little League game with his friend Tommy and Tommy's dad rather than me. When I asked why, he said, 'Cause guys just do stuff different than girls.' That statement made me realize that I couldn't be all things to my son, and that some aspects of sexual identity my son was only going to pick up by being around men."

Authorities generally agree that the best environment for healthy sex role learning is a home in which two parents have a happy, healthy interaction. Although the single-parent home cannot be ideal in this respect, parents need not throw in the towel. Carole Klein writes, "Research into the sexual attitudes of one-parent children concludes that 'inappropriate' attitudes result less from having only one parent than from the attitudes of that parent."[9] By maintaining healthy, open attitudes about both men and women and by enabling their child to have experiences with members of both sexes, the single parent not only facilitates his or her child's learning about sex roles, but makes it clear that these roles, although they do not have to be adhered to rigidly, are important.

In advocating the value of single parents and their single children having extended families, we do not imply that the single-parent home should have a continual parade of people passing through. Instead, the single parent should seek to provide the child and him- or herself easy, natural access to other adults and children who will broaden their perspective on life, strengthen their skills in relating to a variety of people, and in general take the pressure off.

Freedom to Be a Child

Lillian is a widowed mother of one. As she recalled:

> When my husband died, I was overwhelmed with the responsibility that had befallen me. I had to go to work, take care of the car, pay the bills, and take on other responsibilities I'd never had. My son was twelve at the time and very mature, so I began to expect him to do more and more—take care of the lawn, go to the grocery store, help me figure the checkbook, and so on.
>
> At first he seemed to be proud that I was asking him to do the tasks, but then he began to get rebellious—talking back to me, leaving without telling me where he was going—things he never did when his father was alive. I assumed he was acting that way because his father was gone. Finally he was referred to the school counselor because he was misbehaving in school. The counselor said that the rebellion wasn't because of his father's death, but because he resented all the demands I was placing on him. In my grief I'd forgotten that he was still a child and could not take the place of his father.

Lillian's experience is common in cases of divorce as well as death. Dr. Kappelman suggests, "all too often, the only child of divorcing parents finds himself [or herself] in the position of assuming extra responsibilities, extra duties, extra emotional burdens, which are inappropriate and damaging to his emotional growth" and warns that "parents must simply be very careful to avoid transferring roles onto the shoulders of the only child during this stressful and ego-damaging period."[10]

In restructuring family life after the loss of a parent, the remaining parent must also recognize that because there is only one child, it is easy to begin to see that child as a substitute wife or husband (especially if the child is older). To try to make the child a substitute mate is pathologically unhealthy for the child and also prohibits the parent from seeking the adult companionship and support he or she needs to reestablish a satisfying personal life.

Outside Help

Sometimes a single child's greatest need is to have a confidant other than his or her parent. Rather than feeling that this need in the child reflects inadequate parenting, the single father or mother should recognize that the limited size of their family makes it necessary for the child to turn to a third, outside source if a problem involves his or her parent. "When I finally realized I could not be a mother, father, brother, and sister to my child," remarked a single mother of a teen-age daughter, "we got some outside consultation, and I felt an enormous load had been lifted from me. The therapist gave both my daughter and me a neutral third party to talk to."

Often the young child will find the counsel that he or she needs in a sitter or nursery school staffer. For the older child, a teacher, neighbor, relative, or extended family member will be tapped. To this confidant the child will pour out the troubles he or she cannot discuss with parents.

Nora's experience illustrates this point:

> My child was only four when my husband and I separated. We tried very hard not to berate each other around our child and to remain civil when we were together. However, our "civilized" approach didn't allow our son a vent for his anger and resentment toward each of us. Fortunately he had an insightful sitter with whom he'd stayed for two years. Because she was a trusted friend, he talked with her about his feelings and fears (which were expressed mostly in dreams). At first when she told me what he was saying to her I was concerned because he wasn't coming to me with his problems. But I came to realize that he couldn't talk to me because I was a large part of the problem.

When a neutral source is not available to the child, or the child's problems become severe enough to warrant professional help, it is wise to get counseling for the child. The single child must not be left with a feeling that he or she has no one other than his or her parent to turn to. For parents who cannot afford private therapy, mental health facilities that provide counseling service at no or reduced cost are available throughout the country.

Parents Needs

"Everybody talks about the child's needs in a single-parent family, but the parent has needs too," declared a father who had recently been awarded custody of his three-year-old son after a long divorce battle. "As much as I wanted and fought to have my child with me, I cannot sacrifice my whole life for him."

In speaking of the single-parent/single-child situation, many parents strongly emphasize the importance of attending to the adult needs of the parent. "You feel so responsible when you have this one child who looks to you for everything," said one mother, "that you tend constantly to put yourself in second place. That's not healthy for either of you." Some of the needs most often mentioned by parents follow.

Help in Rearing

Every single parent needs help in meeting the day-to-day demands of rearing his or her child. With a young child, the need is for relief from the physical labor of dressing and undressing, feeding, keeping track of, bathing, playing with, answering questions, and tending to "hurts." "When my mother asks what she can do to help," said a single mother with a two-year-old daughter, "I say 'take my kid for a while.' Even an hour helps." Although the physical care requirements lessen as a child gets older, the parent still needs "mental relief."

The parents in our study had been quite inventive about securing the kind and amount of child-rearing relief they felt necessary. In addition to the babysitting or school arrangements parents made to accommodate their job requirements, most had worked out some kind of formal or informal arrangement with friends to assure themselves some "free time." For example, two divorced women who had single daughters aged eight and nine had taken apartments on the same floor of an apartment house so they could easily "exchange kids" without actually living together. The daughters felt perfectly comfortable in either household (they referred to themselves as sisters) and the mothers loved the convenience of having a trusted friend available to take care of their child on the spur of the moment. "I can just tell my daughter I'm going out and she runs over to Lynn's," said one of the mothers. "She's happy and I don't have to make elaborate, week-ahead arrangements. Of course, I do the same for Marge [the other mother]."

In a college family-housing project, four single parents had worked out a rotating schedule with one parent responsible a week at a time for "sitting." That meant that the parent "on duty" could be called on during that week by the other parents to take care of their children. The other parents might not take advantage of the service, but they knew if they needed time away during that week there was someone to care for their child.

What is the pay-off in these arrangements? "Mental sanity," replied one parent. Some parents add that having other children in the household regularly also helps the parent to put his or her single child into better perspective. "Before we started our child care arrangement," said one member of the college students' sitting association, "I really didn't see enough kids in a home situation to know whether my son was behaving normally. Just having some other kids around has helped me see my child more realistically."

In rearing their single child, divorced parents face an additional problem of making sure that both parents maintain a sane relationship with the child. Unless one parent skips out, the separated parents will have to work out arrangements about visiting, gifts, holidays, and such.

With no other child to decentralize the parents' focus, the competition can become fierce, as Marjorie explained: "I thought my husband and I were fairly sensible people until we divorced and started competing for our son's affection. His dad would take him to the circus one weekend, so I'd take him to the ice follies the next. I'd buy him a cowboy outfit; his dad would buy him a bicycle. I'd take him to the orthodontist; his father would take him to the orthopedist. It was an unending race."

For Marjorie, a counselor was successful in interrupting her potentially devastating behavior with Jerry. "The therapist helped me to see what I was doing with Jerry and gave me the courage to think I could stop playing one-upmanship with my former husband without losing my child's affection. Once I stopped playing the game, Jerry's dad did too, and we developed a reasonable relationship with him."

A parental struggle for a child's affection is destined to be destructive for the child. Aside from being spoiled by the material possessions received, the child learns to become a first-rate manipulator, who plays on parents' guilt to get his or her way. Once begun, the cycle often can be broken only by intervention from an outside source, such as a therapist.

Satisfying Employment

Generally a single parent is also a working parent. Unless a widowed parent is independently wealthy or has been left a large estate or a divorced parent is receiving unusually large child support payments, economic necessity dictates that the single parent have a job. But it is not just the money that motivates some single parents to enter the marketplace. "For me a job is an important part of my self-image," said a working mother. "After my divorce, my job success helped me to restore my faith that I was an okay person and gave me the outside contacts I needed to restore my social life."

Single mothers who do have jobs point out that they often confront social criticism. "Society expects that single fathers will work," said Maria, a single mother and an airline ticket agent. "No one ever says the single father is shirking his responsibility by working and raising his kid. But I have people, my mother especially, who tell me that my child is headed for disaster because he's an only child in a one-parent home and has a working mother to boot."

For the single mother who works, research on the effects of a mother's employment on her children is encouraging. Researchers have found that when children of working mothers are compared with children of nonworking mothers—both in early ages and in adolescence—there is no difference.[11] The children of working mothers are not more maladjusted or more likely to be juvenile delinquents, for instance.[12] There is even some evidence that the mother's working may produce a positive effect. In her doctoral dissertation, Kathryn Powell found that children of working mothers, especially girls, were more achievement-oriented than children whose mothers stayed home.[13]

As for the effect of a mother's employment on the relationship she has with her child, again the results seem to be more positive than negative.[14] Working mothers are more likely to express satisfaction with their child than nonworking mothers and less likely to describe their children as burdensome or demanding.[15] Employed mothers also express more contentment with their daily life and work than nonworking mothers, and researchers believe that this may contribute to their positive feelings toward their children.[16]

So the evidence shows that having a parent employed outside the home is not necessarily a detriment to a child. However, there are problems involved in trying to rear a child and maintain a career—as any working parent knows. Although there are the daily hassles of keeping the household in order, parents are generally more concerned about the difficulty of providing adequate care for the child when the parent is at work.

Single mothers and fathers who feel they are handling this problem successfully have some specific suggestions for other parents. The first is to spend the time and money necessary to find a reliable child care arrangement. "I now pay a woman $1.50 per hour to care for my daughter," said one single mother. "That's twice as much as I used to pay a teen-age dropout, and it really puts a crimp in my budget. But the woman is twice as reliable and twice as competent —and that makes it worthwhile."

Parents having school-age children advise not allowing the child to be alone between school dismissal and the parent's arrival home. Their concern is not so much that the child might get into trouble, but that he or she will be lonely. "I was an only child whose mother worked," said a parent of a 12-year-old single child, "so I know how lonely those hours can be. If the kid has a brother or sister, at least there's someone else in the house. My daughter stays with a friend after school, and I pay her friend's mother a small sum each week."

For many single parents, a job is very important (emotionally and financially). Those who feel they may be damaging their child by not being home with him or her can relax. If they have a positive attitude about working and can provide suitable substitute care, their employment should have no ill effects on the child.

Independent Life

A single mother says:

> My son was thirteen when my husband deserted us, and I had to go to work. Because I was away during the day, I felt I had to be home with my son at night. I was afraid he would become a delinquent if I weren't there to monitor his coming and going. So I gave

up any social life of my own. I went to work, came home, and did
whatever my son wanted. What a martyr I was!

In what seemed like a few short years, my son left for college, and
I nearly folded. I had no friends, no adult interests, and no experience in going out on my own. I just didn't know how to do anything
other than work and "mother."

It took quite a while and some real pressure from an understanding minister to get me out of the house and involved in some adult
activities. My advice to single parents with young children is "don't
sacrifice your whole life for them."

One of the recurring problems expressed by single parents
rearing single children is how to be "fair" to the child and
also to maintain a reasonable adult independence. "I feel so
damn guilty when I go out," said one mother. "There's my
poor daughter sitting there, and all I can think about is how I
dropped her off at the sitter at 7:30 a.m., picked her up at
5:30 p.m., rushed home to get her fed and bathed before the
sitter arrived at 7:00 p.m. so I could go out. I always feel like
she's looking at me saying 'who is this person who passes in
and out of my life?' Yet even with all that guilt, I feel I just
have to get away."

Some parents believe that a single child is more resentful
of his or her parent's adult activities because he or she has no
sibling for companionship when the parent goes out. To alleviate the problem, some of these parents allow their child to
have an overnight guest on evenings they are going to be
away. Other parents who have extended friendship networks
try to arrange for the child to stay with these friends.

Perhaps the most troublesome problem for single parents
is how to handle their own relationships with members of the
opposite sex. At some point following death or divorce, most
single parents want to begin dating again. Even when deli-
cately handled, these relationships may be difficult for any
child, and certainly for the single child. Without siblings, the
single child feels very left out when the parent becomes
friends with another adult, and fears of being abandoned by
his or her parent may begin to haunt the child. Dr. Louise

Despert, author of *Children of Divorce*, believes that physical displays of affection between the single parent and another adult can be particularly distressing to a child.[17]

Handling the sensitive issue of male/female relationships is a matter of individual conscience. Some parents we talked with said they simply did not incorporate their opposite-sex friends into their children's lives, except perhaps very casually. For instance, one mother always met her dates away from home, but would introduce her son to a man she was dating if they happened to meet. Other parents believe it is important for the child to know what is going on in the parent's life, so they bring their dates home and discuss with the child the nature of their relationship (acquaintance, friend, very special friend, and such).

The nitty-gritty problem is the sexual relationship. As formerly married adults, some single parents have abandoned traditional ethics about nonmarital sexual relationships. But the question still arises about whether a child should be aware that mother or father "sleeps with" friends. Specifically, should a parent have sex with a friend in the home, and if so, how should the relationship be explained to the child?

Most of the parents with whom we discussed this issue said that they avoided having sex in their home when their child was present. Exceptions were made only late at night when the child was asleep and unlikely to be aware of the activity. The parents acknowledged that limiting sexual relations to these conditions was less than ideal from the adult viewpoint, but they felt it was necessary from the child's standpoint.

Although the question of sexual relationships must be answered by each parent, two points are pertinent to the single child/single-parent situation. First, without siblings, the single child may be particularly threatened by his or her parent's physical involvement with another adult. The single child cannot take comfort in a brother or sister who can provide him or her with companionship (and perhaps mutual misery or fear or anger) while the parent finds companionship with another adult. Being alone in his or her bedroom while mom or dad has a friend in another room can seem grossly unjust to a child.

Second, if the parent has a series of sexual relationships of which the child is aware, the youngster may come to regard such relationships as fairly casual. Casualness about sexual relationships not only provides the child a poor role model for later relationships, but may cause the child to fear that the parent's feeling for him or her is equally as casual. In deciding how they will handle adult relationships, single parents of single children should recognize that their family unit poses some special considerations.

Outside Help

Many authorities believe that a prerequisite for a mentally healthy child is a mentally healthy parent. Although a parent who is mourning the death of a spouse or going through a divorce may be basically emotionally stable, adjusting to his or her new life-style will surely produce periods of anxiety and tension. Even after the initial shock has worn off, lingering effects will be felt. As Jim and Janet Egleson point out, "there is no return to 'normalcy;' the change in the child's [and parents'] life is permanent and has to be absorbed."[18]

The best way a single parent can assure his or her child's sound mental health is to make sure that he or she is "mentally together." For the widowed parent this will require working through the feelings of emptiness and despair that accompany the loss of a spouse. It may also require dealing with the resentment of having been left with the sole responsibility for the child.

In divorce the parent must deal with the emotions of anger, hurt, and guilt that follow the dissolution of a marriage. It is important that the divorced parent confront these feelings so that his or her attitudes (conscious or unconscious) do not negatively color the child's view of male/female relationships. To help minimize the impact of divorce on a child, Dr. Joseph Garai, a professor of psychology, has suggested a number of guidelines, including:

1. Get rid of feelings of hurt, rejection, and resentment. Stop being a man-hater or a woman-hater. Try to develop an optimistic outlook on life.

2. Clarify your attitudes toward sex, love, intimacy, and marriage. Seek competent psychotherapeutic or counseling assistance if you are unable to rid yourself of feelings of rejection. Mobilize your vital energies toward the establishment of rewarding relationships with members of the opposite sex.

3. Let your children (child) know that love is possible, and that sex within the context of a genuinely loving and intimate relationship permits the full experience of growth and joy. Tell children that failure or disappointment in loves does not preclude future success in love and marriage. Stress trust and hope, and discard attitudes of distrust and despair.[19]

It is possible for many single parents to work through the problems of divorce and widowhood with the counsel and support of friends (plus a good deal of personal energy). It may, however, require the professional help of a trained therapist. If you believe that your problems require professional help you should seek a private therapist or call your local mental health clinic.

Remarriage

A parents' divorce or death is a crisis for a child, but there is evidence that remarriage of the remaining parent is at least as or, even more, distressing. In studying 5,000 adolescents, Morris Rosenberg found that children whose mothers remarried appeared to be more disturbed than those whose mothers did not remarry.[20] Dr. Ethelyn Klatskin concluded that as far as adolescents' learning is concerned, "it is more likely to be the remarriage of one or both of the divorced parents rather than a divorce itself which may lead to a disruption in the learning process."[21] Although the absence of a parent leaves the child with a loss, a parent's remarriage presents the child—particularly the single child—with a direct rival.

Dr. Despert suggests that children have mixed feelings about gaining a stepparent. In discussing the single mother who begins bringing her dates home, Dr. Despert writes, "the mother may take it for granted that the child both wants a new father and fears that he may get one."[22] Gaining a stepparent would broaden the family unit—something most children say they want—but at what cost? In the child's eyes, the cost might be losing the mother's or father's attention, and that's a big price to pay for an unknown risk.

Because 80 per cent of all divorced persons remarry, (84 per cent of men and 76 per cent of women), chances are good that a single-parent/single-child family composition will change during the child's at-home years.[23] How can single parents best prepare their child for the possibility of their remarriage?

Carole Klein suggests that a parent slowly introduce a prospective stepparent into the child's life so that the child will have a chance to "gradually develop his [or her] own, hopefully positive, attitudes toward that person."[24] In her conversations with single parents, Klein found "several parents had the idea that it was better to wait until they really liked someone before bringing that person home." But she continues, "they should remember that the level of their involvement will be far ahead of their children's when this happens."[25]

Remarriage of a single-child parent becomes particularly difficult when the marriage partner has children and the single child is suddenly thrust into a multiple-child family. One father who has been through this experience described the transition:

> My future wife and I thought we had carefully prepared my daughter and her children, a daughter and a son, for our marriage.

The kids had spent a lot of time together and seemed really to enjoy each other. Actually my daughter seemed ecstatic to be getting a family.

After the 'honeymoon,' we couldn't believe what started happening. My daughter turned into a whining bitch who did everything she could to turn me against my wife. Her despicable behavior was well matched by that of my wife's kids, who formed an alliance against my daughter and refused even to acknowledge my presence.

Our story has a fairly happy ending. The kids did get so they could live in the same household with about the same degree of tolerance all siblings have for each other, but it wasn't easy.

Neither experienced parents nor family relations experts have any pat answers for single parents who seek to integrate their single child with a new stepparent or ready-made brothers and sisters. The transition seems easiest when adults go slowly, realizing that for children the remarriage of a parent may seem just another adult decision over which he or she has no control. And a single-child parent should remember that because he or she is the child's only "family," the child may be understandably reluctant to share that family. This does not mean that the parent should bend to the child's immediate wishes and forego remarriage—but it does mean that the parent should be sensitive to the child's feelings and take the time needed to assure that the parent's remarriage is as happy an experience for the child as for him or her.

Single Parent/Single Child: A Positive Experience

The world of the single parent/single child is a very special one. It is small, intense, and in many ways limiting for both parent and child. But the family unit need not be a negative experience.

To make the one-parent/one-child family a positive experience, it is necessary that parent and child concentrate on what they *have* rather than what they are *missing*. Their small family may limit the number of relationships they have, but it will allow them to get to know each other better and will heighten their sensitivity to each other's joys and sorrows. Having no third person to act as a buffer in their conflicts, parent and child will learn to work through interpersonal problems. By experiencing life so intimately and intensely, the parent and child can forge a strong, close, trusting, loving bond that will last throughout their lives.

Single parents who are concerned about raising a single child will be refreshed by the conclusion of a single-child adult who was raised by her mother in a one-parent home. "Throughout my childhood," says Marion, "I complained about not having a father and about not having a sister or brother. But now that I'm an adult and look around at peo ple who grew up in 'normal' family situations, I realize my relationship with my mother has been so special that it far outweighed what I missed by not having others in the family."

Notes

Introduction

1. General Science Survey, July 1975, conducted by the National Opinion Research Center, Chicago. Data were based on a random sample of 1,490 noninstitutionalized adults, 18 years and over, in the United States. This figure includes respondents who have no children and want two children, and those who have two children and do not want more. Appreciation is expressed to Dr. Ken Wilson, Assistant Professor of Sociology, East Carolina University, for analyzing all the NORC data used in this book.

2. Ibid. This figure includes respondents who have no children and want one child, and those who have one child and do not want more.

3. *Daily Reflector* (Greenville, N.C.), March 27, 1977, p. 5.

Chapter 1

1. B. F. Skinner in a lecture. Quote repeated to us by Jack Turner, Huntsville-Madison Mental Health Clinic, Huntsville, Alabama, in personal communication, December, 1976.

2. *The Denver Post*, January 23, 1976, p. 62; *Daily Camera* (Boulder, Colorado), February 26, 1976, p. 18.

3. E. E. LeMasters, *Parents in Modern America* (Homewood, Ill.: The Dorsey Press, 1977), p. 31.

4. Kenneth W. Terhune, *A Review of the Actual and Expected Consequences of Family Size* (Washington, D.C.: Government Printing Office, 1974), pp. 174–76.

5. W. Godfrey Cobliner, "Some Maternal Attitudes toward Conception," *Mental Hygiene*, 49 (October 1965), 550–57.

6. Eric K. Erikson, *Childhood and Society* (New York: W. W. Norton, 1963), p. 10.

7. Boyd C. Rollins and Harold Feldman, "Marital Satisfaction over the Family Life Cycle," *Journal of Marriage and the Family*, 32, no. 1 (February 1970), 20–28.

8. Paul C. Rosenblatt, "Behavior in Public Places: Comparison of Couples Accompanied and Unaccompanied by Children," *Journal of Marriage and the Family*, 36, no. 4 (November 1974), 750–55.

9. E. E. LeMasters, "Parenthood as Crisis," *Marriage and Family Living*, 19 (November 1957), 352–55.

10. Everett D. Dyer, "Parenthood as Crisis: A Re-Study," *Marriage and Family Living*, 25 (May 1963), 196–201.

11. Harold Feldman "The Effects of Children on the Family," in *Family Issues of Employed Women in Europe and America*, ed. Andree Michel (Lieden, The Netherlands: E. F. Brill, 1971).

12. Candyce S. Russell, "Transition to Parenthood: Problems and Gratifications," *Journal of Marriage and the Family*, 36 (May 1974), 294–303.

13. Daniel F. Hobbs, "Parenthood as Crisis: A Third Study," *Journal of Marriage and the Family*, 27 (August 1965), 367–72.

14. General Social Science Survey, July 1975, conducted by the National Opinion Research Center, Chicago.

Chapter 2

1. George Gallup, *The Gallup Poll: Public Opinion, 2, 1949–1958* (New York: Random House, 1972), 941.

2. Janet Griffith, "Social Pressure on Family Size Intentions," *Family Planning Perspectives*, 5 (1973), 237–42.

3. Edwin S. Solomon, Jeanne E. Clare, and Charles F. Westoff, "Social and Psychological Factors Affecting Fertility," *Milbank Memorial Fund Quarterly*, 34, no. 2 (April 1956), 160–77.

4. George Gallup, *The Gallup Poll: Public Opinion, 1, 1935–1948* (New York: Random House, 1972), 524.

5. *Daily Reflector* (Greenville, N.C.), March 27, 1977, p. 5

6. General Social Science Survey, July 1975, conducted by the National Opinion Research Center, Chicago.

7. E. W. Bohannon, "The Only Child in a Family," *Journal of Genetic Psychology*, 5 (1898), 475–96.

8. Norman Fenton, "The Only Child," *Journal of Genetic Psychology*, 35 (December 1928), 547.

9. Brenda Ueland, "The Only Child," *Liberty* (December 3, 1927), 32.

10. Florence L. Goodenough and Alice M. Leahy, "The Effect of Certain Family Relationships upon the Development of Personality," *The Pedagogical Seminary and Journal of Genetic Psychology*, 34 (March 1927), 45–51, 69–71.

11. Britomar J. Handlon and Patricia Gross, "The Development of Sharing Behavior," *Journal of Abnormal and Social Psychology*, 59 (November 1959), 425–28.

12. Refia Uğurel-Semin, "Moral Behavior and Moral Judgment of Children," *Journal of Abnormal and Social Psychology*, 47 (April 1952), 463–74.

13. Toni Falbo, "Does the Only Child Grow Up Miserable?" *Psychology Today*, 9 (May 1976), 65.

14. Ruth B. Guilford and D. A. Worchester, "A Comparative Study of the Only and Non-Only Child," *Journal of Genetic Psychology*, 38 (December 1930), 411–26.

15. Morris Rosenberg, *Society and the Adolescent Self-Image* (Princeton, N.J.: Princeton University Press, 1965), p. 103.

16. Dorothy T. Dyer, "Are Only Children Different?" *Journal of Educational Psychology*, 36 (April 1945), 297–302.

17. Kenneth W. Terhune, *A Review of the Actual and Expected Consequences of Family Size* (Washington, D.C.: Government Printing Office, 1974), p. 72.

18. Barbara S. Hazen, *Why Couldn't I Be an Only Kid Like You, Wigger* (New York: Atheneum, 1975).

19. Falbo, "Only Child," p. 65.

20. Merl E. Bonney, "Relationships between Social Success, Family Size, Socio-Economic Home Background, and Intelligence Among School Children in Grades III to V," *Sociometry*, 7 (February 1944), 26–39.

21. Terhune, *Review of Family Size*, p. 77.

22. J. W. B. Douglas, *The Home and the School* (London: Macgibbon and Kee, 1964); Theodore Lentz, "Relation of IQ to Size of Family," *Journal of Educational Psychology*, 18 (October 1927), 486–96; Philip E. Vernon, "Recent Investigations of Intelligence and Its Measurement," *Eugenics Review*, 43 (October 1951), 125–37.

23. "The Only Child Found to Pay a Cognitive Penalty," *Behavior Today*, 7, no. 35 (September 13, 1976), 4.

24. Ibid.

25. Edith A. Davis, "The Mental and Linguistic Superiority of Only Girls," *Child Development*, 8 (June 1937), 139–43.

26. J. P. Lee and A. H. Stewart, "Family or Sibship Position and Scholastic Ability," *Sociological Review*, 5 (July 1957), 94.

27. A. E. Bayer, "Birth Order and College Attendance," *Journal of Marriage and the Family*, 28 (November 1966), 484.

28. Anne Poole and Annette Kuhn, "Family Size and Ordinal Position: Correlates of Academic Success," *Journal of Biosocial Science*, 5 (January 1973), pp. 51–59; Anne Poole, "Bythway's Statistical Trap," *Journal of Biosocial Science*, 6 (January 1974), 73–74.

29. Stanley Schacter, "Birth Order, Eminence, and Higher Education," *American Sociological Review*, 28 (October 1963), 757–68.

30. Maurice O. Burke, "A Search for Systematic Personality Differential of the Only Child in Young Adulthood," *Journal of Genetic Psychology*, 89 (September 1956), 71–84; Fenton, "Only Child," pp. 546–56; H. F. Hooker, "The Study of the Only Child at School," *Journal of Genetic Psychology* 39 (1931), 122–26; John Stuart, "Data on the Alleged Psychopathology of the Only Child," *Journal of Abnormal and Social Psychology*, 20 (January 1926), 44.

31. Albert Ellis and Robert M. Beechley, "A Comparison of Child Guidance Clinic Patients Coming from Large, Medium and Small Families," *Journal of Genetic Psychology*, 79 (September 1951), 131–44.

32. J. A. Levy, "Comparative Study of Behavior Problems in Relation to Family Constellation," *American Journal of Psychiatry*, 10 (1931), 637–54.

33. Falbo, "Only Child," p. 65.

34. Terhune, *Review of Family Size*, p. 80.

35. Norma E. Cutts and Nicholas Moseley, *The Only Child* (New York: G. P. Putnam's Sons, 1954), p. 201.

36. Elizabeth Hurlock, *Child Development* (New York: McGraw-Hill Book Company, 1964), p. 622.

37. Charles McArthur, "Personalities of First and Second Children," *Psychiatry*, 19 (February 1956), 47–54; Helen Koch, "Attitudes of Young Children toward Their Peers as Related to Certain Characteristics of Their Siblings," *Psychological Monographs: General and Applied*, 70, no. 19 (1956), 1–41.

38. Eda J. LeShan, *The Only Child*, Public Affairs Pamphlet No. 293 (New York: Public Affairs Committee, 1960), p. 8.

39. Arthur T. Jersild, *Child Psychology* (Englewood Cliffs, N.J.: Prentice-Hall, Inc., 1968), p. 314.

Chapter 3

1. Walter Toman, *Family Constellation* (New York: Springer Publishing Co., Inc., 1961), pp. 120–21.

2. James H. S. Bossard and Eleanor S. Boll, *The Large Family System: An Original Study in the Sociology of Family Behavior* (Philadelphia: University of Pennsylvania Press, 1956), p. 282.

3. Norma E. Cutts and Nicholas Moseley, *The Only Child* (New York: G. P. Putnam's Sons, 1954), p. 15.

4. Ibid.

5. Alexander R. Doberenz, ed., *The Family Unit: Population Growth Symposium No. 3* (Green Bay: University of Wisconsin, 1972), pp. 132–33.

6. Ibid.

7. Robert B. Reed, "The Interrelationship of Marital Adjustment, Fertility Control, and Size of Family," *The Milbank Memorial Fund Quarterly*, 25 (October 1947), 383–425.

8. Ernest W. Burgess and Leonard S. Cottrell, *Predicting Success and Failure in Marriage* (New York: Prentice-Hall, Inc., 1939), p. 259.

9. Richard O. Lang, "A Study of the Degree of Happiness and of Unhappiness in Marriage as Rated by Acquaintances of the Married Couples" (unpublished master's thesis, University of Chicago, 1932), pp. 49–50.

10. Robert O. Blood and Donald M. Wolfe, *Husbands and Wives: The Dynamics of Married Living* (Glencoe, Ill.: The Free Press, 1960), pp. 262–63.

11. "Summary Report: Final Divorce Statistics, 1971," *Monthly Vital Statistics Report*, 23, no. 8 (November 6, 1974), 3.

12. Eleanor Lewis, "Psychological Determinants of Family Size: A Study of White Middle-Class Couples Ages 35–45 with Zero, One, or Three Children," *Proceedings of the Annual Convention of the American Psychological Association*, 7, pt. 2 (1972), 665–66.

13. F. Ivan Nye, John Carlson, and Gerald Garrett, "Family Size, Interaction, Affect and Stress," *Journal of Marriage and the Family*, 32 (May 1970), 218.

14. Joan K. Lasko, "Parent Behavior toward First and Second Children," *Genetic Psychology Monographs*, 49 (February 1954), 97–137.

15. Charles McArthur, "Personalities of First and Second Children," *Psychiatry*, 19 (February 1956), 47–54.

16. Edwin S. Solomon. Jeanne E. Clare, and Charles F. Westoff, "Social and Psychological Factors Affecting Fertility: Fear of Childlessness, Desire to Avoid an Only Child, and Children's Desire for Siblings," *The Milbank Memorial Fund Quarterly*, 34 (April 1956), 160–77.

17. Irma Hilton, "Differences in the Behaviors of Mothers toward First- and Later-Born Children," in *Child and Adolescent Psychology: A Book of Readings*, eds. Gene R. Medinnus and Ronald C. Johnson (New York: John Wiley and Sons, 1970), pp. 204–18.

18. *Population and the American Future*, Report of the Commission on Population Growth and the American Future (Washington, D.C.: U.S. Government Printing Office, 1972), p. 81.

19. Elizabeth Hurlock, *Child Development* (New York: McGraw-Hill, 1964), p. 662.

20. Bernard Rosen, "Family Structure and Achievement Motivation," *American Sociological Review*, 26 (August 1961), 574–84.

21. Lewis, "Psychological Determinants," p. 666.

22. Ibid.

Chapter 4

1. General Social Science Survey, July 1975, conducted by the National Opinion Research Center, Chicago.

2. Lucille K. Forer, with Henry Still, *The Birth Order Factor: How Your Personality Is Influenced by Your Place in the Family* (New York: David McKay Company, Inc., 1976), pp. 10–13, 45–66.

3. Helen L. Koch, "Attitudes of Young Children toward Their Peers As Related to Certain Characteristics of Their Siblings," *Psychological Monographs: General and Applied*, 70, no. 19 (1956), 1–41, and "Children's Work Attitudes and Sibling Characteristics," *Child Development*, 27 (September 1956), 289–310.

4. Social Science Survey.

5. *Denver Post*, April 18, 1974, p. 22; Judith Blake, "Can We Believe Recent Data on Birth Expectations in the United States?" *Demography*, 11 (February 1974), 25–44; *Youth 1974* (New York: Institute of Life Insurance), p. 61.

6. A. John Arrowood and Donald M. Amoroso, "Social Comparison and Ordinal Position," *Journal of Personality and Social Psychology*, 17, no. 2 (1965), 101–04; Alan E. Bayer, "Birth Order and College Attendance," *Journal of Marriage and the Family*, 28 (November 1966), 480–84; Elizabeth Douvan and Joseph Adelson, *The Adolescent Experience* (New York: John Wiley and Sons, 1966) pp. 277–78; Forer, Still, *Birth Order Factor*, pp. 67–74; Robert D. Palmer, "Birth Order and Identification," *Journal of Consulting Psychology*, 30 (April 1966), 129–35; Edward E. Sampson, "Birth Order, Need Achievement, and Conformity," *Journal of Abnormal and Social Psychology*, 64, no. 2 (January 1962), 155–59.

7. Lucille Forer, *Birth Order and Life Roles* (Springfield, Ill.: Charles C. Thomas Publisher, 1969), pp. 28–42; Stanley Schacter, *The Psychology of Affiliation* (Stanford, Calif.: Stanford University Press, 1959), pp. 42–89; Robert R. Sears, "Ordinal Position in the Family As a Psychological Variable," *American Sociological Review*, 15 (June 1950), 397–401.

8. Forer, Still, *Birth Order Factor*, p. 53.

9. Sampson, "Birth Order," pp. 155–59.

10. Herman Vollmer, "Jealousy in Children," *American Journal of Orthopsychiatry*, 16 (October 1946), 660–71.

11. Social Science Survey.

12. Forer, Still, *Birth Order Factor*, p. 76.

13. Ibid., pp. 57–60.

14. Harry McGurk and Michael Lewis, "Birth Order: A Phenomenon in Search of an Explanation," *Developmental Psychology*, 7, no. 3 (November 1972), 366.

15. James H. Bossard and Eleanor S. Boll, *The Large Family System: An Original Study in the Sociology of Family Behavior* (Philadelphia: University of Pennsylvania Press, 1956).

16. Bossard and Boll, *Large Family*, pp. 311–12.

17. Ibid., p. 221.

18. Bernice M. Moore and Wayne H. Holtzman, *Tomorrow's Parents: A Study of Youth and Their Families* (Austin: University of Texas Press, 1965), pp. 191–214.

19. Bossard and Boll, *Large Family*, pp. 156–66.

20. Ibid., pp. 298, 320.

Chapter 5

1. Albert Rosenfeld, "What Is the Right Number of Children?" *Life*, 71 (December 17, 1971), 99.

2. W. Godfrey Cobliner, "Some Maternal Attitudes towards Conception," *Mental Hygiene*, 49 (October 1965), 550–57.

3. A. H. Maslow and Bela Mittelmann, *Principles of Abnormal Psychology: The Dynamics of Psychic Illness* (New York: Harper and Brothers, 1941), p. 245.

4. Alice S. Rossi, "Family Development in a Changing World," *American Journal of Psychiatry*, 128, no. 9 (March 1972), 1061.

5. Ibid.

6. Jules Henry and Samuel Warson, "Family Structure and Psychic Development," *American Journal of Orthopsychiatry*, 21 (January 1951), 60.

7. Ivan Nye, John Carlson, and Gerald Garrett, "Family Size, Interaction, Affect and Stress," *Journal of Marriage and the Family*, 32 (May 1970), 216–26.

8. Glen Elder, "Structural Variations in the Child Rearing Relationship," *Sociometry*, 25 (September 1962), 241–62.

9. Carmi Schooler, "Childhood Family Structure and Adult Characteristics," *Sociometry*, 35 (June 1972), 255–69.

10. Bernice M. Moore and Wayne H. Holtzman, *Tomorrow's Parents: A Study of Youth and Their Families* (Austin: University of Texas Press, 1965), pp. 162–90.

11. Joe D. Wray, "Population Pressure on Families: Family Size and Child Spacing," *Reports on Population/Family Planning*, 9 (August 1971), 448.

12. Rossi, "Family Development," p. 1058.

13. Genevieve M. Landau, "Why Small Families Are Back in Style," *Parents' Magazine*, 48 (July 1973), 52.

14. Michael L. Masterson, "Family Structure Variables and Need Approval," *Journal of Consulting and Clinical Psychology*, 36 (February 1971), 12–13.

15. P. R. Ehrlich and A. H. Ehrlich, *Population Resources Environment: Issues in Human Ecology* (San Francisco: W. H. Freeman and Company, 1970), p. 1.

16. *Population and the American Future: The Report of the Commission on Population Growth and the American Future* (Washington, D.C.: Government Printing Office, March 1972), p. 19.

17. "The Crucial Math of Motherhood," *Life*, 72 (May 19, 1972), 49.

18. Frederick S. Jaffe, "Low-Income Families: Fertility in 1971–1972," *Family Planning Perspectives*, 6, no. 2 (Spring 1974), 108–10.

19. James A. Sweet, "Differentials in the Rate of Fertility Decline: 1960–1970," *Family Planning Perspectives*, 6, no. 2 (Spring 1974), 107.

20. Ehrlich and Ehrlich, *Population Resources*, p. 38.

21. *Population and the American Future*, p. 163.

22. L. A. Mayer, "U.S. Population Growth: Would Fewer Be Better?" in *The American Population Debate*, ed. Daniel Callahan (New York: Doubleday and Company, 1971), p. 13.

23. *Population and the American Future*, p. 20.

24. "The Crucial Math of Motherhood," p. 49.

25. *Daily Reflector* (Greenville, N.C.), March 27, 1977, p. 5.

26. Judith Blake, "Can We Believe Data on Birth Expectations in the United States?" *Demography*, 11 (February 1974), 25–44.

27. *Youth 1974* (New York: Institute of Life Insurance), p. 61.

28. *The Denver Post*, July 11, 1974, 1AA.

29. Contact the American Association of Marriage and Family Counselors (225 Yale Avenue, Claremont, California 91711) and ask for the names of qualified marriage counselors in your area.

30. Rosenfeld, "What Is the Right Number of Children?" p. 99.

Chapter 6

1. Norma E. Cutts and Nicholas Moseley, *The Only Child* (New York: G. P. Putnam's Sons, 1954), p. 238.
2. Arthur T. Jersild, *Child Psychology* (Englewood Cliffs, N.J.: Prentice-Hall, Inc., 1968), pp. 395–96.
3. Based in part on work of David M. Levy, *Maternal Overprotection* (New York: W. W. Norton and Company, Inc., 1966), pp. 37–112.
4. Murray Kappelman, *Raising the Only Child* (New York: E. P. Dutton, 1975), pp. 127–33.
5. Robert H. Watford, "A Study of Attitudes of Elementary Teachers toward Only Children" (unpublished doctoral dissertation, University of Northern Colorado, 1976), p. 42.
6. "The Only Child Found to Pay A Cognitive Penalty," *Behavior Today*, 7, no. 35, (September 1976), 4.
7. Some signs based in part on the work of Cutts and Moseley, *Only Child*, pp. 117–18.
8. Paul H. Mussen, John J. Conger, and Jerome Kagan, *Child Development and Personality* (New York: Harper and Row, Publishers, 1969), pp. 664–65.

Chapter 7

1. *Standard Education Almanac* (Chicago: Marquis Academic Media, 1975), p. 61.
2. A. E. Bayer, "Birth Order and College Attendance," *Journal of Marriage and the Family*, 28 (November 1966), 484; Anne Poole and Annette Kuhn, "Family Size and Ordinal Position: Correlates of Academic Success," *Journal of Biosocial Science*, 5 (January 1973), 51–59; Anne Poole, "Bythway's Statistical Trap," *Journal of Biosocial Science*, 6 (January 1974), 73–74; Richard A. Rehberg and David L. Westby, "Parental Encouragement, Occupation, Education and Family Size: Artifactual or Independent Determinants of Adolescent Educational Expectations?" *Social Forces*, 45 (March 1967), 362–74; Stanley Schacter, "Birth Order, Eminence, and Higher Education," *American Sociological Review*, 28 (October 1963), 757–68.

3. Toni Falbo, "Does the Only Child Grow Up Miserable?" *Psychology Today*, 9 (May 1976), 60, 65.

4. Maurice O. Burke, "A Search for Systematic Personality Differentiae of the Only Child in Young Adulthood," *The Journal of Genetic Psychology*, 89 (September 1956), 71–84.

5. William D. Altus, "Birth Order and Its Sequelae," *Science*, 151 (January 1966), 44–48; S. Stewart West, "Sibling Configurations of Scientists," *The American Journal of Sociology*, 66 (November 1960), 268–74.

6. "Is First Best?" *Newsweek*, 73 (January 6, 1969), 37.

7. Murray Kappelman, *Raising the Only Child* (New York: E. P. Dutton and Co., Inc., 1975), pp. 175–76.

8. Lucille Forer, with Henry Still, *The Birth Order Factor* (New York: David McKay Co., Inc., 1976), pp. 116–117.

9. Norma E. Cutts and Nicholas Moseley, *The Only Child* (New York: G.P. Putnam's Sons, 1954), pp. 179–81.

10. Ernest W. Burgess and Leonard S. Cottrell, Jr., *Predicting Success or Failure in Marriage* (New York: Prentice-Hall, Inc., 1939), pp. 104–13; Lewis Terman, *Psychological Factors in Marital Happiness* (New York: McGraw-Hill Book Co., 1938), pp. 208–09.

11. Burgess and Cottrell, *Marriage*, pp. 104–13.

12. Kappelman, *Only Child*, p. 182.

13. Eda J. LeShan, *The Only Child*, Public Affairs Pamphlet No. 293 (New York: Public Affairs Committee, 1960), p. 18.

14. Cutts and Moseley, *Only Child*, pp. 201–02.

15. General Social Science Survey, July 1975, conducted by the National Opinion Research Center, Chicago.

Chapter 8

1. "Population Characteristics: Marital Status and Living Arrangements," *Current Population Reports*, U.S. Department of Commerce, Series P-20, no. 255 (November 1973), 2.

2. General Social Science Survey, July 1975, conducted by the National Opinion Research Center, Chicago.

3. Michael McFadden, *Bachelor Fatherhood: How to Raise and Enjoy Your Children as a Single Parent* (New York: Walker and Company, 1974), p. 93.

4. Murray Kappelman, *Raising the Only Child* (New York: E.P. Dutton and Co., Inc., 1975), pp. 166–67.

5. Jim Egleson and Janet F. Egleson, *Parents without Partners: A Guide for Divorced, Widowed or Separated Partners* (New York: E. P. Dutton and Co., Inc., 1961), p. 169.

6. Kappelman, *Only Child*, p. 156.

7. Egleson and Egleson, *Parents without Partners*, p. 168.

8. Hanna E. Kapit, "Help for Children of Separation and Divorce," in *Children of Separation and Divorce*, eds. Irving R. Stuart and Lawrence E. Abt (New York: Grossman Publishers, 1972), p. 212.

9. Carole Klein, *The Single Parent Experience* (New York: Walker and Company, 1973), p. 204.

10. Kappelman, *Only Child*, p. 165.

11. Lee G. Burchinal and Jack E. Rossman, "Relations among Maternal Employment Indices and Developmental Characteristics of Children," *Marriage and Family Living*, 23 (November 1961), 334–40.

12. Ibid., pp. 334–40.

13. Kathryn S. Powell, "Maternal Employment in Relation to Family Life," *Marriage and Family Living*, 23 (November 1961), 350–55.

14. Ronald C. Johnson and Gene R. Medinnus, *Child Psychology, Behavior and Development* (New York: John Wiley and Sons, Inc., 1969), p. 283.

15. F. Ivan Nye, "Adjustment of the Mother: Summary and a Frame of Reference," in *The Employed Mother in America*, eds. F. Ivan Nye and Lois W. Hoffman (Chicago: Rand McNally and Company, 1963), pp. 384–85.

16. F. Ivan Nye, "Personal Satisfactions," in *The Employed Mother in America*, eds. F. Ivan Nye and Lois W. Hoffman (Chicago: Rand McNally and Company, 1963), p. 326.

17. Louise J. Despert, *Children of Divorce* (New York: Doubleday and Company, 1953), p. 57.

18. Egleson and Egleson, *Parents without Partners*, p. 153.

19. Joseph E. Garai, "Sex Education," in *Children of Separation and Divorce*, eds. Irving R. Stuart and Lawrence E. Abt (New York: Grossman Publishers, 1972), pp. 245–46.

20. Morris Rosenberg, *Society and the Adolescent Self-Image* (Princeton, N.J.: Princeton University Press, 1965), pp. 105–106.

21. Ethelyn H. Klatskin, "Developmental Factors," in *Children of Separation and Divorce*, eds. Irving R. Stuart and Lawrence E. Abt (New York: Grossman Publishers, 1972), p. 194.

22. Despert, *Children*, p. 55.

23. "Marriage, Divorce, and Remarriage by Year of Birth: June 1971," *Current Population Reports*, U.S. Bureau of the Census, Series P-20, no. 239 (September 1972), p. 6-7; Paul C. Glick, "A Demographer Looks at American Families," *Journal of Marriage and the Family*, 37 (February 1975), 15–26.

24. Klein, *Single Parent*, p. 173.

25. Ibid.

three / *Appendixes*

I / *Study of Single Children*

The study of single children included 105 subjects ranging in age from 8 to 66. Adult subjects (over age 18) answered 21 questions; children subjects (under age 18) answered 10 questions paralleling those asked adults. Of the total subjects, 52 responded to the questions by completing a questionnaire; the other 53 were personally interviewed, with the questionnaire used as a basis. Subjects' responses are summarized in the following pages.

Survey of Only Children

1. Age

Ages	Percentage
8–16	23%
17–19	4
20s	20
30s	24
40s	20
50s	5
60s	4

2. Sex   Female—62%; male—38%

3. Natural born—96%; adopted—4% (adults)

4. Occupation (adults)

Professional	28%
(doctor, lawyer, teacher, engineer, scientist, etc.)	
Homemaker	22
Secretary	15
Sales	11
Student	8
Unemployed	5
Other (technician, clerk, laborer, machinist, etc.)	11

5. Education (adults)

Less than high school	1%
High school	12
High school +	37
College degree	22
College degree +	28

6. Looking back on your childhood, do you think there were advantages in being an only child? Explain (adults)
   Do you think there are good things about being an only child? Name some (children)

	Total	Adult	Children
Yes	93%	86%	100%
No	7	14	
Explanations			
More possessions, opportunities	34	33	40
More parent attention	30	32	24
Better for personal development	16	13	28
No sibling problems	20	22	8

7. Do you think there were problems in being an only child? Explain. (adults)

Do you think there are bad things about being an only child? Explain. (children)

	Total	Adult	Children
Yes	69%	75%	64%
No	31	25	36
Explanations			
Lack companionship	58	43	73
Parents overfocus, protect, expect, etc.	27	35	20
Personal development retarded	10	20	
Other (no motherhood preparation, holidays lonely, no excitement, etc.)	5	2	7

8. Was there an age or time at which you especially wished you had brothers or sisters? (adults)
   Would you like to have other children in your family? (children)

	Total	Adult	Children
Yes	64%	75%	54%
No	36	25	46

At approximately what age did you wish for a sibling? (adults)

Ages	
6–10	33%
11–18	32
Adult	8
All ages	27

Would you like to have a sister? brother? both?

	Total	Adult	Children
Sister	21%	27%	14%
Brother	37	32	43
Both	42	41	43

Why did you wish for more children in the family at that time? (adults)

Companionship	71%
To lessen parents' focus	15
Other kids were having siblings	14

9. Do you think there were differences between you and your friends
who had brothers and sisters that resulted from your being an only
child? Explain. (adults)
Do you think there are differences between you and your friends who
have brothers and sisters? Describe some of them. (children)

	Total	Adult	Children
Yes	53%	53%	54%
No	47	47	46

Explanations

Personality or behavior differences (maturity, self-confidence, flexibility, etc.)	51	65	38
Family differences (no confidant, no rivalry, etc.)	31	11	50
Parent differences (permissiveness, attentiveness, closeness, etc.)	18	24	12

10. Were your childhood problems different from those of your friends?
(adults)

Yes—35%   No—65%

Explanations

Dependency problems	36%
Problems relating to peers	17
Other (parents more strict, not competitive, no confidant, etc.)	47

11. Do you think other children you knew were particularly aware that
you were an only child? (adults)
Do your friends know that you do not have brothers or sisters? (children)

	Total	Adults	Children
Yes	57%	37%	77%
No	43	63	23

How did they react toward your being an only child? (adults)
Positive reactions (envied, "surprised
  you're an only," etc.)   62%
Negative reactions (pitied, blamed
  misbehavior on onliness, teased
  about being spoiled)   38

Does your being an only make a difference to your friends? (children)

Yes—0%   No—100%

What do they say to you about being an only child? (children)

Say I am lucky, have more advantages   95%
Other (don't you get bored? aren't you lonely? etc.)   5

12. Were your closest friends in childhood often other only children? (adults)
Are any of your best friends only children? (children)

	Total	Adults	Children
Yes	27%	22%	31%
No	73	78	69

13. Did both parents live in the home during most of your childhood? (adults)

Yes—88%   No—12%

14. Was your mother regularly employed outside the home? (adults)

Yes—25%   No—75%

15. Do you think you received more attention from your parents than did your friends who were not only children? (adults)

Yes—73%   No—27%

Do you think the attention was beneficial or harmful? Explain. (adults)

Beneficial (parents encouraged, taught more,
  developed self-confidence, more democratic,
  etc.)   60%
Harmful (overprotective, interfered, magnified faults, emotionally stunting)   12
Both   28

Because you are their only child, do you think your parents treat you differently than other parents treat their children? (children)

Yes—75%   No—25%

In what ways do they treat you differently?

Positive (more attention, more possessions, etc.)   60%
Negative (expect more, more strict)   40

16. As an adult, are there ways you are affected by not having brothers and sisters? Explain. (adults)

Yes—67%   . No—33%

Explanations
Family effects (miss family ties, miss
   confidant, closer to family)   48%
Parent effects (sole responsibility for family,
   closer to parents, parents more interfering)   26
Personal effects (value friends more, ap-
   preciate own children more, more self-
   centered, "feel I've missed something")   26

17. If you are married, how many brothers and sisters does your husband/wife have? (adults)

Number of Siblings	
0	9%
1	41
2	19
3	10
4	6
5	15

18. If you are married (or have been married), does your being an only child seem to have an effect on your marital relationship? Explain. (adults) (84% of adult respondents were or had been married)

Yes—41%   No—59%

Explanations
Problems in compromising   33%
Torn between parents and spouse   11
Other (expect too much attention, like house
   quieter, need more independence, etc.)   56

19. If you have a family of your own, how many children do you have? (adults)

Number of Children	
0	41%
1	14
2	27
3	13
4	2
5	2
6	1

Do you plan to have more children? How many more? (adults) (Information used only to analyze responses of respondents having one child.)

20. If you have no children now but plan to have a family in the future, how many children would you like to have? (adults)
    If you have a family of your own someday, how many children would you like to have? (children)

Number of Children	Total	Adults	Children
0	4%		8%
1	2	3	
2	48	59	38
3	4		8
3 or 4	5	10	
4 or more	4		8
Undecided	33	28	38

21. If you are a parent, do you think that your being an only child has an effect on your relationship with your own children? Explain. (adults)

Yes—61%   No—39%

Explanations

Children's bickering gets on my nerves	21%
Allow my children more independence	16
Developed more open communication	9
Enjoy children's relationships	7
Try not to be too demanding	7
Other (value children more, don't always want kids around, hard to put kids first, etc.)	40

II / *Study of One-Child Parents*

The study of one-child parents included 168 persons. "Younger parents" (those having a child under age 18) answered one set of questions; "older parents" (those having an adult child) answered another set. The questions asked each group were essentially the same, but the wording of some questions differed and parents of adult children were asked an additional question. Of the subjects, 89 were personally interviewed, with a questionnaire used as the basis; 79 gave written responses to the same questionnaire. The one-child parents' responses are summarized in the following pages.

Survey of Parents of Only Children

	Age	Percentage
1. Age of father	20s	8%
	30s	24
	40s	18
	50s	19

60s	13
70s	2
deceased	16

	Age	Percentage
Age of mother	20s	8
	30s	24
	40s	24
	50s	19
	60s	21
	70s	3
	deceased	1

	Occupation	Percentage
2. Father's occupation	Professional (physician, lawyer, teacher, scientist, etc.)	55%
	Business	18
	Laborer	18
	Retired	7
	Student	2

	Occupation	Percentage
Mother's occupation	Homemaker	42
	Professional (teacher, lawyer, writer, accountant, etc.)	38
	Secretary	11
	Student	6
	Retired	3

	Years of schooling	Percentage
3. Father's education	Elementary	10%
	High school	17
	High School +	27
	College degree or more	46

	Years of schooling	Percentage
Mother's education	Elementary	3
	High school	22
	High school +	36
	College degree or more	39

	Age	Percentage
4. Age of child	3–6	18%
	7–12	18
	13–19	18
	20s	24
	30s	16
	40s	3
	50s	3
Sex of child	Male	46%
	Female	54
Natural born	Natural born	96%
Adopted		4

5. How many brothers and sisters do you have?

Number of Siblings	Fathers	Mothers
0	18%	10%
1	22	29
2	25	11
3	12	10
4	6	12
5	5	8
6 or more	12	20

6. Did you have a close relationship with your own brothers and sisters as a child?

	Fathers	Mothers
Yes	83%	90%
No	17	10

Have you been close as adults?

	Fathers	Mothers
Yes	69%	90%
No	31	10

7. Before your child was born, did you have a preference of sex?

Preference	Total	Younger parents	Older parents
Boy	27%	35%	17%
Girl	13	9	17
No preference	60	56	66

8. How long were you married before your child was born?

Years married	Total	Younger parents	Older parents
1	27%	24%	30%
2	9	15	3
3	21	20	21
4–5	19	21	18
6–9	16	15	18
More than 10	8	5	10

9. Why didn't you have more children? (older parents)
   Why haven't you had more children? (younger parents)

Reasons	Total	Younger parents	Older parents
Medical reasons	34%	27%	42%
Didn't want more	23	24	22
Marital problems	10	13	8
Financial problems	10	11	8
"Just didn't happen"	9	4	14
Career interests	4	8	
Other (age, no adoptable babies, emotional coping, war, spouse's death, etc.)	10	13	6

10. Do you plan to have more children? How many more? (Younger parents)

      Yes—3%   No—72%   Maybe—25%

11. Were both parents in the home during your child's first 18 years? (older parents)
Are both parents presently living in the home? (younger parents)

	Total	Younger parents	Older parents
Yes	82%	82%	82%
No	18	18	18

12. Did mother regularly work outside the home when your child was younger? (older parents)
Is mother regularly employed outside the home? (younger parents)

	Total	Younger parents	Older parents
Yes	39%	50%	29%
No	61	50	71

13. Do you think there are advantages in having only one child?

	Total	Younger parents	Older parents
Yes	79%	88%	69%
No	21	12	31
Explain			
Financial	35	31	42
Child gets more attention experience, time	28	32	21
Less demanding for parents	13	7	12
Closer parent-child relationship	8	13	9
Freedom of career for mother	5	8	3
Other (no estate problems, no sibling comparison, parents have more time for each other, etc.)	11	9	13

14. Do you think there are problems in having only one child?

	Total	Younger parents	Older parents
Yes	65%	81%	45%
No	35	19	52
Explain			
Too much attention, protection, focus, etc.	28	26	30
Child lonely	24	21	27
Child misses sibling experience	22	21	23
Parents have to entertain child	5	3	7
Other (parents criticized, feel we've deprived child, etc.)	21	29	13

15. When your child was growing up, did you notice differences between him/her and children who had brothers and sisters that seemed to be the result of his/her being an only child? (older parents)
In comparing your child with children who have brothers and sisters, do you notice any differences that seem to be the result of his/her being an only child? (younger parents)

	Total	Younger parents	Older parents
Yes	42%	47%	38%
No	58	53	62
Explain			
More mature	19	16	23
Slower social development	14	16	12
More comfortable with adults	12	8	18
Less aggressive	10	12	6
Better vocabulary	7	12	0
Other (less demanding, more popular, less scheming, less sharing, more resourceful, etc.)	38	36	41

16. Do you think there were ways in which your child was more mature

than his/her friends who had brothers and sisters? (older parents)
Do you think there are ways in which your child is more mature than
his/her friends who have brothers and sisters? (younger parents)

	Total	*Younger parents*	*Older parents*
Yes	70%	59%	79%
No	30	41	21
Explain			
More independent, resourceful, responsible	30	23	35
More adultlike	23	8	35
Better vocabulary	14	15	13
Understands adults better	12	27	
More leadership ability	5		10
Other (more creative, more compassionate, quieter, etc.)	16	27	7

17. Do you think there were ways in which your child was less mature than
his/her friends who had brothers and sisters? (older parents)
Do you think there are ways in which your child is less mature than
his/her friends who have brothers and sisters? (younger parents)

	Total	*Younger parents*	*Older parents*
Yes	29%	35%	24%
No	71	65	76
Explain			
Socially	30	12	71
More self-centered	13	19	
Less responsible	9	13	
Less flexible	9	13	
Other (less competitive, less careful of money, more timid, etc.)	39	43	29

18. Now that your son/daughter is an adult, do you notice any differences
between him/her and other adults who have brothers and sisters that
seem to be the result of his/her being an only child? (older parents)

Yes—20%   No—80%

Explain

More independent, realistic, self-sufficient	34%
More selfish, insecure	33
Other (misses family ties, more anxious to have own child, etc.)	33

19. Was there a time or age in your child's life when being an only child seemed to be a problem for him/her? If so, when and why? (older parents)
Has there been a time or age in your child's life when being an only child seemed to be a problem for him/her? If so, when and why? (younger parents)

	Total	Younger parents	Older parents
Yes	42%	47%	37%
No	58	53	63
When?			
Preschool	29	33	22
Elementary	37	67	
Junior High	10		22
Adolescence	24		56
Why?			
Peers having siblings	44	56	50
Desired companions	48	44	38
Other (interested in family, parents divorcing, etc.)	8		12

20. Do you foresee a time in the future when being an only child may present problems for your child? (younger parents)

Yes—30%
No—70%

If so, when?
Adulthood—100%

21. In raising your child, did you purposely do any special things because he/she was an only child? If so, explain by the following age groups: (older parents)
In raising your child, have you purposely done any special things

because he/she is an only child? If so, explain by the following age
groups: (younger parents)

	Total	*Younger parents*	*Older parents*
Yes	72%	67%	78%
No	28	33	22

Preschool age	*Total*
Provided companions	29%
Sent to preschool	24
Encouraged activities	16
Read to	12
Spent time with, played with	9
Other (more toys, voice in choosing sitter, emphasized sharing)	10

Elementary school age	*Total*
Encouraged, provided friends	39%
Encouraged group experiences	32
Encouraged overnight visits	12
Took other child when traveling	7
Other (gave allowance, sent to private school, etc.)	10

Adolescence	*Total*
Provided experiences	36%
Encouraged friends	25
Didn't indulge	11
Other (provided a pet, encouraged hobbies and group activities, etc.)	28

22. Did (or does) your child attend preschool?

Yes—82%   No—18%

Was it beneficial?
Yes—100%

How?
Socialization	61%
Academic preparation	20
Relationship with another adult	5

Child gained confidence 5
Other (new insights for parents, gave child
  independence from home, increased
  competitiveness, etc.) 9

23. Now that your child has reached adulthood, do you treat him/her differently than you would if there were other children in the family? (older parents)

Yes—26%   No—74%

Explain
All concern is still for child 50%
More generous with child 33
Other (more anxious about child,
  worry more about my old age, etc.) 12

24. What specific suggestion for rearing would you give to other parents of only children?

Older parents	*Total*
Provide playmates	26%
Give love, attention	20
Don't spoil, overindulge	14
Don't smother	11
Develop independence	9
Other (be thankful for him/her, let child be child, treat responsibly, etc.)	20

Younger parents	*Total*
Provide companions	21%
Don't overfocus	18
Mother should have other activities	15
Treat as if he/she had siblings	6
Expose child to many situations	6
Other (get a dog, don't overreact to wants, let child share in family decisions, etc.)	34

25. Over the years, have there been people who have been critical of you for having an only child? (older parents)
Are there people who are critical of you for having only one child? (younger parents)

	Total	Younger parents	Older parents
Yes	56%	58%	55%
No	44	42	45

Were (are) critics mainly friends or relatives?

	Total	Younger parents	Older parents
Friends	47%	31%	61%
Relatives	12	13	11
Both	41	56	28

What kinds of comments did (do) they make?

	Total
It's not "fair" to the child	31%
Child will be lonely	13
Child will be spoiled	13
Other (who'll keep you in your old age, "one is nothing," why don't you adopt, it's a shame, etc.)	43

How did (do) you respond to these comments?

	Total
Ignore them	38%
Tell them it's none of their business	19
Tell them off	13
Other (God sent us what he wanted, happy to have this one, etc.)	30

26. Have there ever been people who have expressed approval of your one-child family? What kind of comments did they make? (older parents)
    Are there people who express approval of the one-child family? If so, what kind of comments do they make? (younger parents)

	Total	Younger parents	Older parents
Yes	58%	65%	50%
No	42	35	50

(Responses too diverse to categorize)

27. If you were starting your family today, how many children would you wish to have?

Number of Children	Total	Younger parents	Older parents
0	8%	13%	3%
1	23	25	21
2	40	30	50
1 or 2	8	17	
2 or 3	6		13
3	10	9	10
4	5	6	3

28. Would you recommend the one-child family to other couples?

	Total	Younger parents	Older parents
Yes	41%	39%	43%
No	25	23	27
Qualified "yes"	7		15
"I wouldn't give that advice"	27	38	15

III / Study of Fathers: Their First Year

The following questionnaire was completed by 102 first-time fathers. Special appreciation is extended to Dr. Richard Gilman, Associate Professor of Sociology at East Carolina University, for analyzing the data in this study.

Fatherhood—The First Year

This questionnaire is designed to find out your reaction to your first baby. Please answer each question as though you were discussing your experiences with a prospective father and friend who has asked you, "What is it really like?" Select the best single answer and add qualifications in the margin if necessary. Thank you.

Your Baby

1. *Check the age closest to your first baby*

    (2%) One month or younger   (12%) Three months
    (5%) Two months   (15%) Four months

(9%) Five months   (12%) Nine months
(9%) Six months   (4%) Ten months
(8%) Seven months   (5%) Eleven months
(12%) Eight months   (9%) Twelve months
                                   (0%) Thirteen months or older

Average age—slightly over six-and-a-half months.

2. *Sex of baby:*

         (55%) Boy   (45%) Girl

Preparation for the Baby

3. Was this baby planned in the sense that both you and your wife wanted to become parents *as soon as possible?*

         (69%) Planned   (31%) Unplanned

4. If you checked the unplanned answer in the previous question, did you want this baby to be born? *Not answered properly.*

(1%) No
(7%) Mostly yes
(30%) Definitely yes

5. Please state your personal reason (independent from your wife's reason) for having your baby. Most frequent responses included:

I have always wanted a child.
I wanted a child that was part of my wife and me.
To carry on my name.

6. Did you participate in any parenthood classes before the baby was born?

         (33%) Yes   (65%) No   (2%) None available

7. Did you and your wife attend natural childbirth or Lamaze classes before the baby was born?

         (27%) Yes   (71%) No   (2%) None available

8. Did you ever feed or change the diapers of someone else's baby before your baby was born?

         (59%) Yes   (41%) No

9. Did any male (father, brother, or friend) ever talk with you about how he played with, talked to, fed, enjoyed, or did not enjoy babies before your baby was born?

(20%) No   (54%) Occasionally   (26%) Several times

10. Was this talk primarily? *Not answered properly.*

   (1%) Negative
   (28%) Positive
   (55%) Equally positive and negative
   (   ) Answered "No" for No. 9

11. Before your baby was born, what sex child did you want?

   (19%) Really wanted a boy
   (42%) Preferred a boy
   (32%) Really didn't care
   (7%) Preferred a girl
   (0%) Really only wanted a girl

Care of the Baby

12. Did your wife have anyone (other than yourself) to help her with the baby when she came home from the hospital?

   (74%) Yes   (26%) No

13. How long did this person help on a systematic basis after your wife came home from the hospital? *Not answered properly.*

   (   ) Less than two weeks
   (   ) Three weeks
   (   ) Four weeks
   (   ) Six weeks
   (   ) Longer than eight weeks

14. During the last week, how many times have you fed the baby? *Not answered properly.*

   (   ) None (baby breast fed)
   (   ) None (baby bottle fed)
   (8%) Once
   (14%) Twice
   (15%) Three times
   (34%) Four to six times
   (11%) Seven to twelve times
   (5%) Thirteen to twenty times
   (1%) More than twenty times
   Average number of times = five.

15. During the last week, how many times have you changed the baby's diapers?

(19%) None   (17%) Four to six times
(8%) Once   (20%) Seven to twelve times
(8%) Twice   (7%) Thirteen to twenty times
(14%) Three times   (7%) More than twenty times

Average = slightly over five-and-a-half times per week.

16. During the last twenty-four hours, how many times has your wife complained about the baby?

( ) None   ( ) Three times
( ) Once   ( ) Four times
( ) Twice   ( ) Five times
     ( ) Six times or more

Not answered properly.

17. Has a physician told you that your baby has colic?

(20%) Yes   (80%) No

18. Is the baby (9%) breast fed or (84%) bottle fed now?

Your Feelings about the Baby

19. How much do you wish that you and your wife could return to the time before the baby was born?

(73%) None   (25%) Some   (2%) A great deal

20. How would you describe your feelings toward the baby?

( ) Hate
( ) Mild negative feelings
( ) Indifference
( ) Mild positive feelings
(15%) Love
(85%) Love plus extreme happiness

21. Have your feelings changed since the baby was born?

(41%) Yes   (59%) No

22. If so, in what way?
Majority said that their feelings of love had increased.

Working Wife

23. When your wife got pregnant, was she working?

   (23%) Not at all
   (10%) Part-time
   (67%) Full-time

Social Life and Religious Preference

24. On the average, how many times each week did you and your wife go out to eat, see a movie, take a drive, etc. before the baby was born?

   (4%) No times per week
   (26%) Once per week
   (29%) Two times per week
   (25%) Three times per week
   (10%) Four times per week
   (6%) Five or more times per week
   Average—slightly over two times per week.

25. On the average, how many times each week do you and your wife go out to eat, see a movie, take a drive, etc. now?

   (15%) No times per week
   (38%) Once per week
   (31%) Two times per week
   (13%) Three times per week
   (3%) Four times per week
   (   ) Five or more times per week
   Average—one-and-a-half times per week.

26. Which of the following comes closest to your present religious preference?

   (3%) Agnostic/atheist
   (68%) Protestant
   (3%) Roman Catholic
   (1%) Jew
   (0%) Unitarian
   (0%) Morman
   (25%) Other (specify:)

Sleep

27. How many times in the last week have you gotten up at night to take care of the baby?

(62%) None   (2%) Four times
(12%) Once   (2%) Five times
(14%) Twice   (5%) Six or more times
(3%) Three times
Average—once per week.

28. Does the baby sleep in the room with you and your wife?

(20%) Yes   (72%) No   (8%) Sometimes

Marriage

29. Rate your marital happiness prior to your wife's pregnancy.

1	2	3	4	5
Terrible		Average		Great

30. Rate your marital happiness during your wife's pregnancy.

1	2	3	4	5
Terrible		Average		Great

31. Rate your marital happiness since the baby's birth.

1	2	3	4	5
Terrible		Average		Great

Computer analysis of these variables indicated that 75% of the fathers felt that their baby had no effect on their marriage; 20% felt that their marital relationship had improved; 3% felt that their relationship had become worse. (2% did not answer this question.)

In-laws

32. Rate the level of your satisfaction with your in-laws prior to the birth of the baby.

1	2	3	4	5
Terrible		Average		Great

33. Rate the level of your satisfaction with your in-laws now.

1	2	3	4	5
Terrible		Average		Great

Computer analysis indicated that 85% of the fathers said that their in-law relationship had not changed since the baby's birth; 10% reported that their relationships had improved. (5% did not answer the question.)

Parents

34. Rate the level of your satisfaction with your parents prior to the birth of the baby.

1	2	3	4	5
Terrible		Average		Great

35. Rate the level of your satisfaction with your parents now.

1	2	3	4	5
Terrible		Average		Great

85% of the fathers reported that the relationship with their parents had not changed since the baby; 10% reported that the relationships had improved. (5% did not anwer this question.)

Background Information

36. When were you born?
37. When did you marry?
38. What level of education have you completed?

    (4%) Grade school
    (26%) Some high school
    (28%) Finished high school
    (32%) Some college
    (3%) Finished college
    (7%) Graduate school
    (0%) Finished graduate school

39. Are you currently:

    (85%) Working full-time?
    (3%) Working part-time?
    (5%) Looking for work?
    (0%) Keeping house?
    (7%) Going to school?

40. What is your occupation? Please state your job title and the kind of place at which you work. For example, "I am a cashier at Nichols, which is a discount department store."
41. What is your wife's occupation now? Please state her job.
42. What is your present family income (including spouse's income or that of parents if you live at home)? (2% did not answer.)

    (3%) Less than $5,000
    (15%) Between $5,000 and $7,499
    (16%) Between $7,500 and $9,999
    (47%) Between $10,000 and $14,999
    (14%) Between $15,000 and $19,999
    (3%) Between $20,000 and $24,999
    (   ) Between $25,000 and $29,999
    (   ) Between $30,000 and $39,999
    (   ) $40,000 or more

43. What is your race?

    (7%) Black
    (93%) White
    (0%) Indian
    (0%) Other (specify:

IV / Study of Mothers with Two Children

The following questionnaire was completed by 245 mothers. Special appreciation is extended to Dr. Ken Wilson, Assistant Professor of Sociology at East Carolina University, for analyzing the data in this study.

Mothers with Two Children

Dear Parent:

This questionnaire has been designed to assess your feelings as a mother of two children as compared to when you had only one child. Your desire for privacy and anonymity will be respected. There is no way to trace your identity.

Your First Child

1. Check the category that describes the age of your first child.

(36%) Under age 5
(37%) Between 6 and 17
(27%) Over age 18

2. Was your first baby planned in the sense that you wanted to become a mother *as soon as possible*?

(60%) Planned   (40%) Unplanned

3. If you checked the unplanned answer in the previous question, did you want your first child to be born?

(3%) No   (15%) Mostly yes   (82%) Definitely yes

4. Sex of the first child.

(51%) Male   (49%) Female

5. Did your first child have any serious physical defects?

(3%) Yes   (97%) No

6. How did one child affect your career?

(44%) It didn't interfere; I don't want a career.
(8%) It has made it very difficult.
(48%) It hasn't made much difference.

7. If you checked either of the last two answers for question 10, please explain.

8. Rate your marital happiness prior to the pregnancy with your first child.

1	2	3	4	5
Terrible		Average		Great

9. Rate your marital happiness during the pregnancy with your first child.

1	2	3	4	5
Terrible		Average		Great

10. Rate your marital happiness after the birth of your first child and before the pregnancy with the second child.

1	2	3	4	5
Terrible		Average		Great

From before the first pregnancy to after the birth of the first child, 12% of the

mothers reported that their marriages got worse, 71% reported that their mar-
riages stayed the same; 17% reported that their marriages improved.

Your Second Child

11. When did you decide to have two children?

    (42%) Before I had any children.
    (36%) After I had one child.
    (22%) Didn't decide—it just happened.

12. If you checked "didn't decide" in the last question, did you want your second child to be born?

    ( ) Yes   ( ) No   (data not available)

13. Please put numbers in the parentheses below to indicate, in order, the first three reasons you had a second child: 1 = first and most important reason, 2 = second and next most important reason, etc. Write 0 if you never considered this reason.

    ( )   Parents expressed desire for more grandchildren.
    (8%)   My husband wanted a second child.
    ( )   Had second child so that first child would not be solely burdened with us when we are old.
    (6%)   First child was a girl; wanted another girl.
    ( )   First child was a boy; wanted another boy.
    (8%)   Fulfillment as a person.
    (45%)   Really enjoyed first child; wanted another to repeat the experience.
    ( )   First child asked us for a brother or sister.
    (29%)   Wanted a companion for first child.
    ( )   First child was a girl; wanted a boy.
    ( )   First child was a boy; wanted a girl.
    ( )   Only children are spoiled children.
    ( )   Only children are lonely children.
    ( )   Friends would consider us odd if we had only one child.
    ( )   By having two children, we would have one left if one died.

    Specify other reasons not listed above.
    Other reasons included: Our second child was not planned; it just happened. I was remarried and wanted to have a child with my new husband. My first child had a birth defect so I tried to have another because my doctor assured me that a second child could be normal.

14. Check the closest age to your second child.

    (59%) Under age 5
    (22%) Between 6 and 17
    (19%) Over age 18

15. Sex of second child

    (44%) Male   (56%) Female

16. Check the age difference between your first and second child.

    (5%) One year   (20%) Four years
    (26%) Two years   (7%) Five years
    (26%) Three years   (16%) More than five

17. Did your second child have any serious physical defects?

    (4%) Yes   (96%) No

18. How mucn do you wish that you and your spouse could return to being a one-child family?

    (94%) None   (6%) Some   (0%) A great deal

19. How would you describe the amount of work two children require (dressing, feeding, laundry) as opposed to the amount one child requires?

    (6%) Two are just as easy as one.
    (70%) A little more work, but not much.
    (22%) Double the work.
    (2%) Triple the work.

20. How would you describe the amount of time two children require as opposed to the amount one child requires?

    (2%) More time to myself after second child was born.
    (37%) Not much difference between one and two children.
    (44%) Less time to myself after second child was born.
    (17%) A great deal less time to myself after second child was born.

21. How would you describe the amount of noise (crying, children playing, children arguing) between having one and having two children?

    (19%) No difference
    (3%) Less noise
    (64%) More noise
    (14%) A great deal more noise

22. Was the effect of the first child on you personally greater than the effect of the second child?

   (45%) Yes   (30%) No   (25%) No difference

23. How would you describe your feelings as a mother?

   (61%) I love it.
   (3%) I feel trapped.
   (32%) I enjoy it.
   (3%) I wish I had a career.
   (1%) I am indifferent.

24. How has having two children affected your pursuing a career?

   (39%) It hasn't; I don't want a career.
   (11%) It has made it very difficult.
   (50%) It hasn't made much difference.

25. If you checked either of the last two answers to question 29, please explain.
26. Please state in your own words how having two children differs from having one.
   "There is more adjustment from none to one than from one to two" best summarizes the difference between having one and two children as reported by these mothers.

Husband

27. How would you describe your husband's feelings as a father?

   (6%) He is too involved in his work to be aware of the children and their needs.
   (89%) He loves children.
   (1%) He doesn't like children.
   (3%) He is indifferent.
   (1%) He wishes we didn't have children.

28. How would you describe your husband's participation in child care responsibilities?

   (23%) We share the responsibilities equally.
   (17%) He does 40%; I do 60%.
   (27%) He does 30%; I do 70%.
   (17%) He does 20%; I do 80%.
   (16%) He does 10%; I do 90%.

(   ) He does 60%; I do 40%.
(   ) He does 70%; I do 30%.
(   ) He does 80%; I do 20%.
(   ) He does 90%; I do 10%.

29. Did your husband want to have the first child?

(96%) Yes   (4%) No

30. Did your husband want to have a second child?

(92%) Yes   (8%) No

Religious Preference

31. Which of the following comes closest to your present religious preference?

(5%) Agnostic/atheist
(76%) Protestant
(5%) Roman Catholic
(1%) Jew
(2%) Unitarian
(1%) Morman
(10%) Other (specify)

Marriage

32. Rate your marital happiness prior to your second child.

1	2	3	4	5
Terrible		Average		Great

33. Rate your marital happiness during your pregnancy with your second child.

1	2	3	4	5
Terrible		Average		Great

34. Rate your marital happiness since the birth of your second child.

1	2	3	4	5
Terrible		Average		Great

From before the second pregnancy to the birth of the second child, 14% of the mothers reported that their marriages got worse; 77% reported that their marriages remained the same; 9% reported that their marriages improved. Summarizing the effect of both children on their marriage, from before the first pregnancy until after the birth of the second child, 17% reported that their marriages got worse; 65% reported their marriages stayed the same; 18% reported their marriages improved.

Background Information

35. When were you born?
36. When did you marry?
37. Birth date of first child
38. Birth date of second child
39. What level of education have you completed?

   (0%) Grade school
   (3%) Some high school
   (32%) Finished high school
   (27%) Some college
   (21%) Finished college
   (7%) Graduate school
   (10%) Finished graduate school

40. Are you currently:

   (32%) Working full-time?
   (13%) Working part-time?
   (3%) Looking for work?
   (51%) Keeping house?
   (1%) Going to school?

41. What is your occupation? Please state your job title and the kind of place at which you work. For example, "I am a cashier at a discount department store."
42. What is your husband's occupation? Please state place at which he works.
43. What is your present family income (including spouse's income, or that of parents if you live at home)?

   (2%) Less than $5,000
   (10%) Between $5,000 and $7,499
   (11%) Between $7,500 and $9,999
   (24%) Between $10,000 and $14,999
   (27%) Between $15,000 and $19,999

(12%) Between $20,000 and $24,999
(6%) Between $25,000 and $29,999
(6%) Between $30,000 and $39,999
(2%) $40,000 or more.

44. What is your race?

(2%) Black   (98%) White   (0%) Indian
(0%) Other (Specify)

Please write the name and address of another mother of two children whom you believe would be willing to complete this questionnaire.
Name:

Address:

THANK YOU.

V / Study of Individuals with Siblings

The following questionnaire was completed by 130 college students (46 males, 84 females).

Survey of Individuals Who Have One or More Siblings

This questionnaire is designed to explore your feelings about having brothers or sisters. Your desire for privacy and anonymity will be respected. There are no "right" answers. Please answer the way you feel.

1. Your age *(Average age of the respondents was 19)*
2. Sex *(65% female, 35% male)*
3. Natural born or adopted *(98% natural born, 2% adopted)*
4. Occupation *(Student)*
5. Total years of schooling *(Average—14)*
6. How many brothers do you have? *(72% had at least one brother)*
7. How many sisters do you have? *(71% had at least one sister)*
8. What is the age difference between you and the sibling whose age is closest to yours? *(Average—3 years)*
9. Is the sibling referred to in #8 a brother or sister? *(55% were brothers, 45% sisters)*

10. Looking back on your childhood, what were the advantages in having siblings and in not being an only child? *(39%—playmate, 33%—companion, 20%—someone to share with, 20%—a helper and protector; 13% of the males and 24% of the females listed "helper and protector" as an advantage)*

11. How would you describe the problems associated with having brothers and sisters? *(26%—jealousy; 22%—arguments and fighting; 14%—lack of privacy; all 14% were females; 10%—rivalry and jealousy; 8%—fewer material things)*

12. Was there an age or time at which you especially wished that you did not have brothers or sisters—you wished you were an only child? Yes (39%) No (61%) Approximately what age? *4%—under age 5; 37%—ages 5–10; 48%—ages 11–15; 11%—over age 15)*

13. Was there an age or time at which you especially wished that you had more brothers or sisters? Yes (55%) No (45%) Approximately what age? *(7%—under age 5; 24%—ages 5–10; 39%—ages 11–15; 30%—over age 15)*

14. Would you like to have had more sisters?　　More brothers?
    Both?　　*(Not answered properly)*

15. If you answered "yes" for number 13, why did you wish for more children in the family at the time? *17% of the respondents who answered "yes" to #13 wanted more children in the family because of their positive feelings about a large family; 19% wanted a same-sex companion; 18% just wanted a sibling; 24% wanted an older sibling for a helper; 7% gave other reasons.*

16. Do you think there were differences between you and your friends who were only children? Yes (62%) No (38%) Please explain: *Of the "yes" responses, 44% thought only children were spoiled, selfish, and wanted their own way. Others said they were lonelier (6%); or had more material things (8%).*

17. What special problems of the only child did you observe in your friends who were only children? Please explain: *Essentially the same responses as # 16.*

18. Do you think that other children who knew you were aware that you had brothers and sisters? Yes (91%) No (9%)

19. If you answered "yes" to 18 above, did they react differently to you because you had siblings? Yes (21%) No (79%) Please explain: *Responses too varied to categorize.*

20. How many close friends do you have who are only children?

None—30%	Two or three—2%
One—29%	Four—4%
Two—12%	Five—3%
Three—10%	More than five—4%

Very few—3%   No answer—3%

21. How many close friends do you have who have siblings? *(28%—five or fewer; 72%—over five or many)*
22. Did both your parents live in the home during your childhood? Yes (92%) No (8%)
23. Was your mother regularly employed outside the home? Yes (42%) No (58%)
24. Do you think you received more attention from your parents than did your brothers and sisters? Yes (25%) No (75%)
25. If you answered "yes" to #24, do you think the attention was beneficial or harmful? *53%—beneficial; 15%—harmful; 32%—both or neither.* Please explain. *Reasons too varied to categorize.*
26. As an adult, are there ways that you are affected by having brothers and sisters? Yes (70%) No (24%) No answer (6%) Please explain: *15%—negative effects such as resentment, responsibility, etc., 53%—beneficial effects such as close family ties; someone to turn to, etc.; 38%—answered improperly or not at all.*
27. If you are married (or have been), how many brothers and sisters does your husband/wife have? *Nine respondents were married. Their spouses had the following number of siblings:*

   One sibling—4
   Two siblings—2
   Three siblings—2
   Four siblings—1

28. If you are married (or have been married), does your having siblings seem to have an effect on your marital relationship? Yes (67%) No (33%) Please explain. *All who answered "yes" felt that the effect was positive.*
29. If you have a family of your own, how many children do you have? *The nine married respondents had a total of six children. 33-1/3% had children; 33-1/3% had no children; 33-1/3% did not answer.* Do you plan to have more children? *4—yes; 1—no; 1—maybe; 3—no answer.* How many more? *One more—1; two more—1; two or three more—1; no answer—6.*
30. If you have no children now but plan to have a family in the future, how many children would you like to have?

   None or one   —   2%
   One or two   —   2%
   Two   — 40%
   Two or three —   6%
   Two to four   —   2%
   Three   —   8%

Three or four— 1%
Four — 3%
Four or five — 2%
Five — 2%
No answer — 32%

31. If you are a parent, do you think that your having siblings has an effect on your relationship with your own children? Please explain: *Only three of the 130 respondents were parents. Two of the three answered "yes" to this question.*

32. Do you feel that it is better to have siblings or to be an only child? Please explain: *88%—better to have siblings; 11%—no answer; 1%—not sure which is best. The reasons given were those already detailed in question 10—having siblings provides a playmate and companion, and teaches one to share and get along better with others.*

VI / Association
for the One-Child Family

For years the large family was revered in America. Now the two-child family has become our ideal, and nonparenting has gained a certain acceptance. But the one-child family—the obvious compromise between no children and two children—is still an option not seriously considered by most ·prospective parents.

Why?

Probably because deeply rooted stereotypes about the personalities of only children and the motivations of parents who have one child prejudice couples against a one-child decision.

The time has come re-examine such prejudices. In a world which can no longer afford a single unwanted child, it is time for parents to stop feeling they must have a second child "to save their first" or to assure themselves a "real" parenting experience.

The Association for the One-Child Family, AOCF, has been formed to make the one-child family a more respected and popular family style in our society. Founded by persons having both personal and professional commitment to the one-child family, the Association aims to:

1. Stimulate public interest in and support for the one-child family
   —as an important dimension in world population control
   —as a desirable life style for today's society.

2. Offer psychological support to couples who have one child by choice.
3. Encourage research on single children and one-child families.
4. Confront and challenge prejudicial ideas about the personalities of only children and the motivations of one-child parents.

If you are interested in the one-child family, please join us in AOCF. You will begin receiving the AOCF Newsletter and notification of local chapters being formed around the country. Like other nonprofit organizations, AOCF depends on contributions for its work. Won't you include a tax-deductible contribution with your membership request? Write to Sharryl Hawke, Educational Resources Center, 855 Broadway, Boulder, Colorado 80302.

Index